# PELVIC INFLAMMATORY DISEASE

Anthrax

Antibiotic-resistant Bacteria

Avian Flu

Botulism

Campylobacteriosis

Cervical Cancer

Cholera

Ebola

Encephalitis

*Escherichia coli* Infections

Gonorrhea

Hantavirus Pulmonary Syndrome

*Helicobacter pylori*

Hepatitis

Herpes

HIV/AIDS

Infectious Fungi

Influenza

Legionnaires' Disease

Leprosy

Lyme Disease

Lung Cancer

Mad Cow Disease (Bovine Spongiform Encephalopathy)

Malaria

Meningitis

Mononucleosis

Pelvic Inflammatory Disease

Plague

Polio

Prostate Cancer

Rabies

*Salmonella*

SARS

Smallpox

*Streptococcus* (Group A)

*Staphylococcus aureus* Infections

Syphilis

Toxic Shock Syndrome

Tuberculosis

Tularemia

Typhoid Fever

West Nile Virus

DEADLY DISEASES AND EPIDEMICS

# PELVIC INFLAMMATORY DISEASE

Judith A. O'Donnell, M.D. and
Steven P. Gelone, Pharm. D.

FOUNDING EDITOR
The Late I. Edward Alcamo
Distinguished Teaching Professor of Microbiology,
SUNY Farmingdale

FOREWORD BY
David Heymann
World Health Organization

CHELSEA HOUSE
PUBLISHERS
An imprint of Infobase Publishing

*Dedicated to Ed Alcamo*

**Pelvic Inflammatory Disease**

Chelsea House
An imprint of Infobase Publishing
132 West 31st Street
New York NY 10001

**Library of Congress Cataloging-in-Publication Data**

O' Donnell, Judith A.
   Pelvic inflammatory disease / Judith A. O' Donnell.
         p. cm.
   ISBN 0-7910-8507-4
   1. Pelvic inflammatory disease—Juvenile literature.   I. Title.
   RG411.036         2005
   618.1—dc22                              2005021241

Chelsea House books are available at special discounts when purchased in bulk quantities for businesses, associations, institutions, or sales promotions. Please call our Special Sales Department in New York at (212) 967-8800 or (800) 322-8755.

You can find Chelsea House on the World Wide Web at http://www.chelseahouse.com

Series design by Terry Mallon
Cover design by Keith Trego

Printed in the United States of America

Bang EJB 10 9 8 7 6 5 4 3 2 1

This book is printed on acid-free paper.

All links and web addresses were checked and verified to be correct at the time of publication. Because of the dynamic nature of the web, some addresses and links may have changed since publication and may no longer be valid.

# Table of Contents

# Foreword

In the 1960s, many of the infectious diseases that had terrorized generations were tamed. After a century of advances, the leading killers of Americans both young and old were being prevented with new vaccines or cured with new medicines. The risk of death from pneumonia, tuberculosis (TB), meningitis, influenza, whooping cough, and diphtheria declined dramatically. New vaccines lifted the fear that summer would bring polio, and a global campaign was on the verge of eradicating smallpox worldwide. New pesticides like DDT cleared mosquitoes from homes and fields, thus reducing the incidence of malaria, which was present in the southern United States and which remains a leading killer of children worldwide. New technologies produced safe drinking water and removed the risk of cholera and other water-borne diseases. Science seemed unstoppable. Disease seemed destined to all but disappear.

But the euphoria of the 1960s has evaporated.

The microbes fought back. Those causing diseases like TB and malaria evolved resistance to cheap and effective drugs. The mosquito developed the ability to defuse pesticides. New diseases emerged, including AIDS, Legionnaire's, and Lyme disease. And diseases which had not been seen in decades re-emerged, as the hantavirus did in the Navajo Nation in 1993. Technology itself actually created new health risks. The global transportation network, for example, meant that diseases like West Nile virus could spread beyond isolated regions and quickly become global threats. Even modern public health protections sometimes failed, as they did in 1993 in Milwaukee, Wisconsin, resulting in 400,000 cases of the digestive system illness cryptosporidiosis. And, more recently, the threat from smallpox, a disease believed to be completely eradicated, has returned along with other potential bioterrorism weapons such as anthrax.

The lesson is that the fight against infectious diseases will never end.

In our constant struggle against disease, we as individuals have a weapon that does not require vaccines or drugs, and that is the warehouse of knowledge. We learn from the history of science that "modern" beliefs can be wrong. In this series of books, for example, you will learn that diseases like syphilis were once thought to be caused by eating potatoes. The invention of the microscope set science on the right path. There are more positive lessons from history. For example, smallpox was eliminated by vaccinating everyone who had come in contact with an infected person. This "ring" approach to smallpox control is still the preferred method for confronting an outbreak, should the disease be intentionally reintroduced.

At the same time, we are constantly adding new drugs, new vaccines, and new information to the warehouse. Recently, the entire human genome was decoded. So too was the genome of the parasite that causes malaria. Perhaps by looking at the microbe and the victim through the lens of genetics we will be able to discover new ways to fight malaria, which remains the leading killer of children in many countries.

Because of advances in our understanding of such diseases as AIDS, entire new classes of antiretroviral drugs have been developed. But resistance to all these drugs has already been detected, so we know that AIDS drug development must continue.

Education, experimentation, and the discoveries that grow out of them are the best tools to protect health. Opening this book may put you on the path of discovery. I hope so, because new vaccines, new antibiotics, new technologies, and, most importantly, new scientists are needed now more than ever if we are to remain on the winning side of this struggle against microbes.

David Heymann
Executive Director
Communicable Diseases Section
World Health Organization
Geneva, Switzerland

# 1

# Jennifer's Story

## TROUBLING PAIN

Jennifer woke up again in the middle of the night with the pain. She was beginning to worry about all of the symptoms she was experiencing. The pain in her lower abdomen had been present for almost a week now. When she told her roommate Kiera about it last week, they had decided it was probably all of the fast food and snacks they had been living on as they finished their end-of-semester papers and studied for final exams. But the pain was not getting better, even though Jennifer had been much more careful about her diet. For the past day and a half, she went back and forth between feeling hot and sweaty and getting chills afterwards. The chills were so uncomfortable that she had to put on an extra sweater.

Jennifer had never felt this kind of pain before, not even 12 years ago, when she was 11 and her parents took her to the hospital with belly pain, nausea, and vomiting, which the doctors diagnosed as appendicitis. The pain was different now; it was dull but always there and seemed to be somewhere deep inside her abdomen. The most alarming of all was that the pain was getting worse.

Kiera noticed how uncomfortable Jennifer looked and pulled out the thermometer they had in their medicine cabinet to take Jennifer's temperature. The thermometer was a little hard to read, but they finally agreed that it said 101.2 degrees. Kiera suggested that Jennifer make an appointment at the Student Health Clinic on campus that morning, but Jennifer did not want to miss her sociology exam, so she decided she could wait one more day.

## MORE DISTRESSING SYMPTOMS

When Jennifer returned from her exam, it was dinnertime. When Kiera asked Jennifer what she would like to eat, Jennifer said she felt even more nauseated than she had been feeling all through the test. Jennifer decided to go to bed, hoping that the next day everything would be better and she wouldn't have to see the doctor at the Student Health Clinic.

Jennifer awoke in pain and shivering at 3:00 A.M. Despite an extra blanket, she was soaked in sweat and her teeth were chattering. When she sat up, she felt an intense wave of nausea overcome her, and she ran to the bathroom—just in time to vomit into the sink. Jennifer slowly poured herself a glass of water, and crawled back into her bed. She could not fall back asleep. The pain in her stomach and lower abdomen were awful, and now she had a headache. At 7:00 A.M., she called the Student Health Clinic to get their hours and hopefully make an appointment. Kiera awoke soon after and told Jennifer that she was really worried about her. She agreed to take Jennifer to the clinic as soon as it opened at 9:00 A.M.

## A VISIT TO THE CLINIC

Jennifer felt a little better as she and Kiera waited in the lobby of the Student Health Clinic. The kind older woman behind the receptionist's desk had been friendly and helpful. She assured them that Jennifer would be seen quickly, since many students had already left the campus for their winter break. Jennifer was relieved. She would finally get an answer and the doctor would be able to give her some medicine to make her feel normal again. When the nurse called Jennifer to come back to an examination room, Jennifer stood up and felt dizzy. Then the nausea came back in a second, more severe wave. Kiera helped Jennifer steady herself, but Jennifer had to throw up again. The nurse and Kiera guided her to the closest bathroom. Then, after she had vomited, they walked her to the examination room and helped her lay down on the table. Jennifer could not believe how horrible she felt. The nurse took Jennifer's temperature, and then measured her blood pressure and heart rate. The nurse seemed a bit concerned as she measured Jennifer's blood pressure. She asked Jennifer if she had been eating and drinking, and Jennifer had to admit that she had taken in only some toast and soda over the last two days.

Jennifer was relieved to see a female doctor enter the room. Dr. Hogan introduced herself and asked Jennifer several different questions about her pain and other symptoms. Jennifer described to the doctor where the pain was and how it was different from appendicitis. She explained the fevers, chills, and sweats, and then they talked about the nausea and vomiting. Jennifer was a little surprised when Dr. Hogan began asking about Jennifer's boyfriend, and she was even more surprised when she asked Kiera to step out of the room. Yes, she had a boyfriend. And, yes, they were sexually active. "What could that possibly have to do with my pain?" Jennifer wondered. Dr. Hogan wanted to know when Jennifer and her boyfriend last had sex, and if they had used a condom or any birth control. Jennifer felt scared and confused, and wondered if Dr. Hogan thought she was pregnant even though she had been on a birth control pill for the past two years and was diligent about taking it at the same time every day. However, Jennifer knew that birth control pills are not 100 percent effective, and pregnancy could occur. Jennifer quickly explained this to Dr. Hogan, and added that she had just had a normal period 10 days ago—right before her pain started. Jennifer also explained that, because of all of the work they had been doing in preparation for final exams, Jennifer and her boyfriend had not had sex in weeks.

## THE EXAMINATION AND DIAGNOSIS

Jennifer was shocked by what Dr. Hogan said next. Dr. Hogan explained that the lower abdominal pain, fevers, nausea, and vomiting could be due to a sexually transmitted infection. Even if Jennifer had no discharge from her vagina, this could all be due to something Dr. Hogan called pelvic inflammatory disease, or PID for short. Dr. Hogan indicated that after she fully examined Jennifer's lungs, heart, and abdomen, she would like to perform a pelvic exam. The pelvic exam would allow Dr. Hogan to see if Jennifer's cervix, the bottom part of her uterus, was red and inflamed. The exam would also allow Dr. Hogan to examine Jennifer's ovaries and fallopian tubes to see if they were the source of Jennifer's pain. Jennifer had had a pelvic exam once before when she went to a gynecologist at a clinic near her home; it was part of the process she went through when she was first prescribed birth control pills. It had not been a very pleasant experience. The doctor had been kind, but when the cold metal instrument called a speculum was inserted into her vagina, she felt physically uncomfortable. Jennifer really wanted to know what was wrong with her, so she agreed to have the pelvic exam. Jennifer asked if Kiera could return to be there for support, and Dr. Hogan agreed that that might be very helpful.

As Dr. Hogan pressed down on Jennifer's lower right abdomen, Jennifer could feel the pain worsen. During the pelvic examination, Jennifer nearly jumped off the table when Dr. Hogan felt her cervix and ovary on the right side. Dr. Hogan took some samples during the pelvic exam and told Jennifer the results of the tests should be available in two to three days.

Dr. Hogan then suggested something else: Jennifer should have a blood test to see if she had been exposed to sexually transmitted diseases (STDs) like syphilis or acquired immune deficiency syndrome (AIDS). Dr. Hogan explained that when a person has one STD, they may also have others, and the only way to know is to do screening tests for them. Jennifer agreed to have the blood tests done and signed a consent form. A short time later, the nurse came in to draw her blood. The last test Dr.

Hogan wanted to perform was a urine pregnancy test, just to be certain that Jennifer was not pregnant. Dr. Hogan stepped out to read the pregnancy test and to look at some of the samples she had taken under the microscope. When she returned, she told Jennifer the pregnancy test was negative.

Dr. Hogan confirmed that Jennifer's signs, symptoms, and test results were almost certainly due to PID. She prescribed three different medications as soon as Jennifer was dressed. The first would be an injection of an antibiotic into Jennifer's buttock. The second would be another antibiotic that Jennifer would have to take for 14 days. The third was ibuprofen for the pain. Just as important as the medications, Jennifer would have to tell her boyfriend about the PID so he could come to the clinic for treatment. Dr. Hogan advised Jennifer not to have sex until she had completed therapy and her boyfriend had also been fully treated. Dr. Hogan also told Jennifer that she was very dehydrated, probably due to the fever, low intake of fluids, and vomiting. She suggested Jennifer drink lots of fluids, and if she could not keep down the medicine, she should call the clinic, because she may need to be admitted to the hospital. Dr. Hogan then advised that if Jennifer did not feel better after three days of treatment, she should come back, because it could be a sign that there was an abscess (an accumulation of pus that results from an infection) or some other complication. Otherwise, Dr. Hogan would see her in two weeks, and would call her within the next two to three days with her test results.

**ON THE MEND**

Kiera took Jennifer back to their dorm suite and offered to pick up her prescriptions at the local pharmacy. Jennifer made some tea and got into bed. She could still not believe what Dr. Hogan had said. How could she have an STD? She had only had two other partners besides her current boyfriend, Matt, and as far as she knew they had been an exclusive couple. Many questions swirled in Jennifer's mind: Might Dr. Hogan have been wrong?

Was Matt cheating on her? How was she going to tell him? Kiera returned and Jennifer took her first doses of medications. She then called her professor to see if she could get an extension on her final remaining paper. The professor agreed. When she finally had enough courage to phone Matt, he was unavailable.

Two days later, Jennifer began feeling a lot better. The pain was nearly gone. The fevers and sweats had stopped within a day of taking the medicines. Her appetite was much better. When the phone rang, Jennifer felt nauseous again, afraid that it might be Matt saying he was on his way over to talk. Instead, Jennifer heard Dr. Hogan's voice on the other end of the phone line. Dr. Hogan was pleased to hear how much better Jennifer was feeling, and she then said she had some of Jennifer's test results. Jennifer's test for chlamydia was positive. The test for gonorrhea was negative. Dr. Hogan explained that chlamydia was a bacterium that was most commonly associated with PID. The medications Dr. Hogan had prescribed were working to cure the chlamydia infection and it was important to take the full 14 days of therapy to be sure there would be no relapse. The syphilis blood test was negative, and the HIV blood test was still not back. Dr. Hogan reassured Jennifer that this was typical and that she would definitely have the result when Jennifer returned in another week for her next visit.

## A KNOCK AT THE DOOR AND A FOLLOW-UP VISIT

Someone was at the door. When Jennifer opened it, she saw Matt. He was really concerned about her and wanted to know if she was feeling better and what the doctor had thought was wrong. Jennifer was really nervous, but slowly explained how sick she had been, what Dr. Hogan had said, and what the test results had proved. Matt looked confused, upset, and concerned all at the same time when he heard the news. He reassured Jennifer that he had not been with any other sexual partners since they began their relationship. But Matt was confused about something: How could he have chlamydia when he felt absolutely fine? Jennifer explained what she had learned from Dr. Hogan as well as from searching the topic on the Internet. Many sexually transmitted infections cause no symptoms. People feel fine and never know they have been infected, in some cases until it is too late. Matt agreed to go to the Student Health Clinic to be tested and treated.

When it was time for Jennifer's follow-up appointment at the Student Health Clinic, she was feeling like herself again. Dr. Hogan had additional news to lift Jennifer's spirits: Her HIV test was negative. After examining Jennifer again, Dr. Hogan assured her that everything was normal. Then she and Jennifer discussed another surprising and concerning issue about PID. Dr. Hogan explained that once a woman has had PID, the inflammation in the fallopian tubes caused by the infection can sometimes lead to scarring, and that scarring can make it difficult for the woman to get pregnant. Jennifer was shocked and upset to hear this. Dr. Hogan further explained that the chances of this happening are probably no more than 10 or 15 percent, but she suggested that Jennifer always remember to tell her doctors in the future that she had had PID. Jennifer left the clinic feeling better, but concerned that this one episode of PID could potentially cause her problems for years to come. Jennifer knew she had learned one important lesson from all of this: She would always practice safe sex, and she would make sure she was never infected with an STD again.

# 2

# The ABCs of Pelvic Inflammatory Disease

## A: ANATOMY OF PELVIC INFLAMMATORY DISEASE

The female genital tract is made up of lower and upper segments. The lower segment of the female genital tract includes the labia (the flesh surrounding the opening to the vagina), the vagina itself, and the cervix, which is the lower portion of the uterus. The upper female genital tract consists of the ovaries, where hormones and eggs are produced; the fallopian tubes, which are the tubes that carry eggs from the ovaries to the uterus; and the uterus (also called the womb). The area where the ovaries sit and where the tips of the finger-like extensions of the fallopian tubes are located is sometimes called the **adnexa**. The term "pelvic inflammatory disease" refers to the fact that several parts of the upper female genital tract, all of which are located in the pelvis, may be infected either at once or separately.

When a woman has pelvic inflammatory disease, or PID, she may have an infection that involves any or all of the uterus, the fallopian tubes, and the ovaries. PID can severely damage the fallopian tubes, ovaries, and tissues in and around the uterus and ovaries. The damage can be permanent and may lead to several short- and long-term complications. Some women with PID may also have evidence of lower genital tract infection as well. It is important to understand that the infection always begins in the lower genital tract and ascends to the upper genital tract over time. Frequently, women with lower genital tract infections do not have any symptoms and therefore do not seek care. It is the **asymptomatic** (showing no symptoms) nature of these infections that allows the bacteria

(*continued on page 19*)

## FEMALE ANATOMY PRIMER

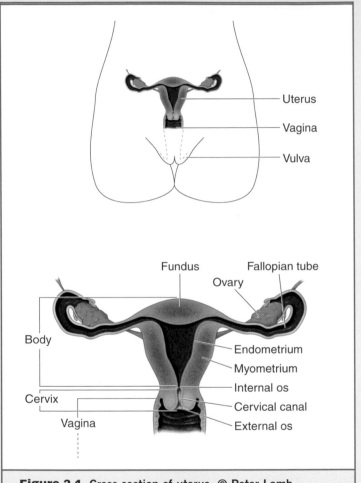

Uterus

Vagina

Vulva

Fundus   Fallopian tube

Ovary

Body

Endometrium

Myometrium

Internal os

Cervix

Cervical canal

Vagina

External os

**Figure 2.1** Cross section of uterus. © Peter Lamb

### LOWER GENITAL TRACT (STARTING WITH THE EXTERNAL STRUCTURES AND WORKING INWARD)

The perineum is a term used to describe the external genital area; it includes the urethra (canal and opening through which urine is excreted from the bladder), labia, and space between the opening of the vagina and the rectum. The labia consist of folds of tissue that surround the opening to the vagina, separated into the outermost folds or labia majora, and the inner folds or labia minora. The vagina is a body cavity that serves to connect the uterus to the external world and through which a baby travels during the birthing process. Menses (the menstrual flow) are excreted through the vagina during the monthly menstrual period. The cervix is located at the bottom of the uterus. The cervix has an opening (the os) and is made up of two different types of cells located in the ectocervix, or the outermost portion of the cervix, and the endocervix, or inner portion of the cervix. It is the cells of the endocervix that are targets for infection by the STDs gonorrhea and chlamydia.

**UPPER GENITAL TRACT**

The uterus is an organ that is normally the size of a fist, but can grow to many times its size during pregnancy to accommodate a full-term baby. The uterus is made up of a thick wall and a cavity, or open area, lined with tissue. Each month the lining of the uterus undergoes changes due to hormones in preparation for receiving a fertilized egg. When it does not receive a fertilized egg, the lining is shed and excreted from the vagina (menses).

There are two fallopian tubes that extend from the top of the uterus toward the ovary on each side. The ends near the ovaries have finger-like extensions called fimbriae that "grab" an egg when it is expelled from the ovary. The ovary is an organ that makes hormones and eggs for fertilization. The fallopian tubes serve to transport the egg to the uterus. The areas on the right and left sides of the female pelvis that contain the ovary and fimbriae of the fallopian tubes are called the adnexa.

**TERMS USED TO DESCRIBE INFECTION INVOLVING THE FEMALE GENITOURINARY TRACT STRUCTURES**

Urethritis is an inflammation of the urethra that causes burning and pain with urination. Vaginitis is an inflammation of the vagina; both infectious and non-infectious conditions may cause vaginitis, and not all infections of the vagina are sexually transmitted. The most common infectious cause of vaginitis is yeast, and yeast infections are not an STD. Women with vaginitis may complain of a discharge from the vagina, pain within the vagina, burning and itching sensations, and pain with intercourse.

Cervicitis is an inflammation of the cervix and is usually caused by an infectious disease. Many women with cervicitis have no symptoms. Women who do have symptoms may complain of a vaginal discharge (although they will not be able to tell from where the discharge is emanating), bleeding, and pain during intercourse.

Endometritis is an inflammation of the lining and walls of the uterus; this is usually due to an infection, though not always an STD. Women who have just delivered a baby can develop endometritis in the immediate postpartum period. In these circumstances, the infection is not caused by an STD, but by other bacteria that contaminated the area during the labor and delivery. Women with endometritis usually experience fever, abdominal pain, and other signs of infection.

Salpingitis is an inflammation of the ovaries and fallopian tubes caused by an infection; women with salpingitis do not always have symptoms.

(*continued from page 15*)

involved to eventually enter the upper genital tract and cause infection there. Even when the infection has moved into the upper genital tract, the woman may only have mild or nonspecific symptoms—in this situation, the PID is described as "silent PID." Women with silent PID continue to have inflammation as a result of the untreated infection in their upper genital tract, and over time, this inflammation can cause scarring of the fallopian tubes. When the fallopian tubes become scarred, they are no longer patent or open, and eggs cannot travel to the uterus. Scarring in the fallopian tubes causes the woman to be infertile, or unable to become pregnant. PID is an important cause of **infertility** (inability to produce children) in women in the United States.

## B: BIOLOGY AND BACTERIOLOGY OF PELVIC INFLAMMATORY DISEASE

What infections cause PID? And how do the organisms that cause the infection get to the genital tract and cause the inflammation? Many different bacteria may cause infection of the female genital tract, but the most common causes of PID are gonorrhea and chlamydia. Gonorrhea and chlamydia are the two most common bacterial sexually transmitted infections in the United States. Another group of bacteria, called anaerobic bacteria or **anaerobes**, also play a prominent role in the development of PID and other pelvic infections.

Gonorrhea is caused by ***Neisseria gonorrhoeae,*** a bacterium that grows well in environments that are warm and moist, like the cervix, uterus, and other upper genital tract organs. Infection and inflammation of the cervix is called **cervicitis**, and, as noted above, it can occur without symptoms. *Neisseria gonorrhoeae* can also infect and multiply in the **urethra** (urinary canal), throat, eyes, rectum, and anus of both women and men. In men, the bacterium can also infect the **epididymis**, the small organ that sits above the testicles and through which sperm travels from the testicles to the penis.

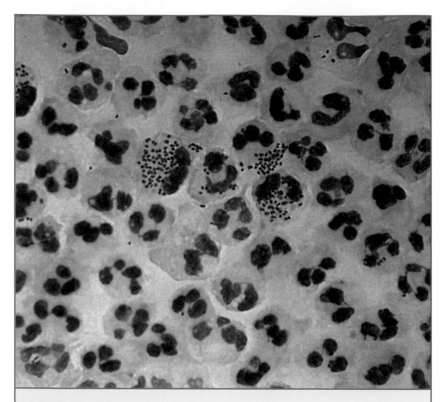

**Figure 2.2** Gonococcal urethritis. Courtesy of Public Health Image Library (PHIL), CDC

When *Neisseria gonorrhoeae* infects these other areas of the body, it usually causes symptomatic disease such as **urethritis** (swelling and inflammation of the urethra). The symptoms of urethritis in men include a white, yellow, or green discharge from the penis, and a burning sensation when urinating. In women, urethritis may cause burning with urination and some discharge from the urethra, though it is usually not as dramatic as in men. *Neisseria gonorrhoeae*, when inoculated into the pharynx during oral sex, causes pharyngitis (sore throat). Gonorrhea may also affect outer tissues lining the eye (**conjunctivae**) causing **conjunctivitis**, or a red eye with yellow or green discharge. In this case, *Neisseria gonorrhoeae* is usually inoculated into the eye from the hand of a patient with gonococcal urethritis, or it has splashed into the eye of a healthcare worker during examination of a patient with gonorrhea. Gonorrhea may also cause **proctitis**, which is inflammation of the rectal tissues that is associated with pain, discharge, and painful bowel movements. Individuals with proctitis have acquired gonorrhea in their rectum in one of two ways. Either they have had receptive rectal intercourse or, in women, the bacteria may actually travel from the vagina or cervix to the rectal canal and infect the cells that make up the lining of the rectum. In men, gonorrhea can rarely ascend into and infect the epididymis, causing **epididymitis**. Men who develop this complication have pain, swelling, and redness of one testicle or one side of their scrotum.

Chlamydia is caused by **_Chlamydia trachomatis_**, a bacterium that infects the cells that make up the cervix, uterus, and other upper genital tract structures in women. It can also infect the urethra, eye, anus, and rectum of both men and women. Chlamydia, unlike gonorrhea, cannot infect the pharynx. It can, like gonorrhea, also infect the epididymis, causing epididymitis in men. *Chlamydia trachomatis* multiplies within the cells it infects. More often than not, chlamydia is an asymptomatic infection in both men and women. Its silent nature in women can lead to spread of the infection from the cervix in the lower genital tract to the upper genital tract and fallopian tubes, and over time cause scarring and infertility, as previously described.

Adolescent and adult women become infected with gonorrhea or chlamydia through unprotected sexual intercourse. The first site of infection with gonorrhea or chlamydia is the cervix. PID occurs when the bacteria ascend from the cervix into the uterus, fallopian tubes, and/or ovaries. As noted, chlamydial or gonococcal infection of the cervix is often unrecognized by the infected woman, due to only mild symptoms or no symptoms at all. Once the bacteria that cause chlamydia or

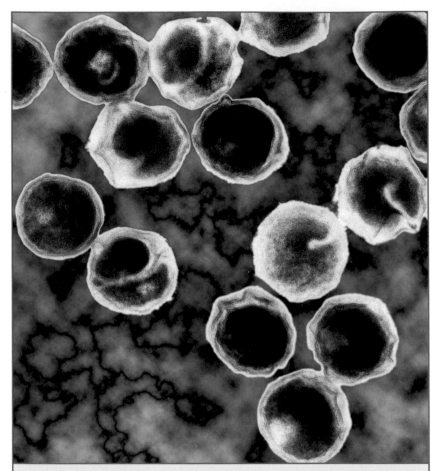

**Figure 2.3** Chlamydia bacteria. © Dr. David Philips/Visuals Unlimited

gonorrhea move into the upper genital tract organs and infect these structures, the infection can still be minimally sympto-matic or silent in many women. However, in women who do develop symptoms of PID, symptoms can be mild, moderate, or severe, as in the case of Jennifer.

The anaerobes that cause PID are several different species of bacteria that live in the gastrointestinal tract and the vagina of humans. Aerobic bacteria require the presence of oxygen to grow and thrive, whereas anaerobic bacteria grow in the absence of oxygen. The presence of oxygen can kill an anaerobic bacterium. Anaerobes can be part of the normal bacteria, or **flora**, that live on or in the human body. Under certain circumstances, however, these anaerobes can also cause infection and disease in the human body. Specifically, anaerobes, when collected together in a closed space, can develop into an abscess. In PID, anaerobes that are part of the normal flora of the female vagina can ascend into the upper genital tract, along with the bacteria that cause chlamydia or gonorrhea. Once there, these otherwise harmless anaerobes can cause infection, inflammation, and in some instances abscess formation of the uterine wall, ovaries, or surrounding areas.

## C: CLINICAL PRESENTATION OF PELVIC INFLAMMATORY DISEASE

Women with PID may be asymptomatic, may present to their physician with a variety of different symptoms, or may only come to the attention of a healthcare provider when they are unable to become pregnant. Asymptomatic PID, or silent PID, has no hallmark of its clinical presentation and is therefore often missed. Because there are no symptoms of the infection, physicians are taught that it is appropriate to screen for certain sexually transmitted infections, like gonorrhea and chlamydia, in specific patient populations, to try to identify infected individuals.

When a woman has symptoms caused by PID, those symptoms may be quite variable. Some women will have only minor complaints. Examples of these may include some nausea, occasional mild lower left- or right-sided abdominal discomfort, mild discomfort during sexual intercourse, or occasional bleeding or spotting that occurs outside of menses (the shedding of the uterine lining during menstruation). Additionally, young women may notice an occasional yellow discharge. Because many of these symptoms can be caused by other diseases, and because they may only be intermittent in nature, it is easy to understand why a woman may not seek the advice of a physician about her complaints. Moreover, not all symptoms will be present in all women. Some women will only have nausea, for example, whereas another woman may have nausea and abdominal discomfort.

Different women may present at the doctor's office or clinic with a different subset of the symptoms described above. It should be noted that women with PID often do not complain of vaginal discharge. When discharge is present, it actually comes from the cervix and the lower genital tract infection (cervicitis) caused by the infecting bacteria; however, women will not know this and will therefore tell their physicians that it is a vaginal discharge. In many women with PID, however, cervicitis will not be prominent, as the bacteria have often left the lower genital tract to ascend into the upper genital tract organs.

Some women with PID are very ill and will come to the office, clinic, or emergency department seeking relief from the severe symptoms they are experiencing. Such patients may have a high fever, persistent nausea and vomiting, and severe abdominal pain in lower and upper sections, and generally appear very uncomfortable. Some women with severe PID may also have an ovarian abscess as a complication of PID. In this case, the woman will have severe pain and swelling on the affected side, and a mass can be felt on examination of the abdomen and affected ovary. In rare instances, an abscess may rupture, spilling pus inside its cavity into the abdomen. This complication requires immediate surgery, much like a ruptured appendix.

# 3

# A Silent Disease: The Diagnosis and Management of PID

## PHYSICAL AND PELVIC EXAMINATION

When PID is being considered as a potential diagnosis, the patient must have a thorough gynecological examination, including both an internal pelvic examination and a bimanual examination. The internal pelvic examination requires the woman to be in the **lithotomy position**—that is, with her feet in stirrups on either side of the examination table and her knees spread apart. An instrument called a speculum is inserted into the vaginal canal, and gently opened so that the vaginal canal and cervix may be viewed. Once the cervix is visible, the examiner evaluates it for redness, swelling, ulceration, or the presence of pus or other liquid discharge emanating from the cervical os (the opening into the cervical/uterine canal that leads up into the cavity of the uterus). The examiner may then obtain swab specimens from the cervix that can be tested as part of the diagnostic process of making the diagnosis of PID and specifically to determine whether the patient has chlamydia or gonorrhea. While the speculum is in place and the cervix is in view, a **Papanicolaou (Pap) smear** of the cervix may also be performed. This test is done by gently scraping the cervix for cells. The cells are sent to a laboratory, where a trained **pathologist** (a doctor who specializes in diagnosing diseases by studying cells and tissues) looks for abnormal cells that could become cancerous. The Pap smear is an excellent screening test for cervical cancer. Once the examination is

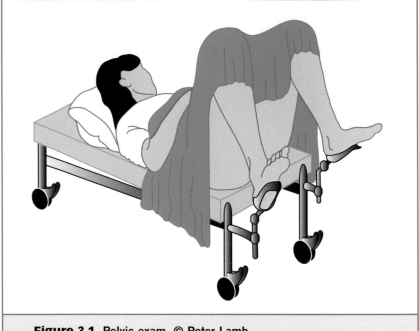

**Figure 3.1** Pelvic exam. © Peter Lamb

complete and any needed samples are obtained, the speculum is removed.

The bimanual examination is the second portion of the gynecological examination. The physician applies a small amount of lubricating jelly onto his or her fingers, and then inserts the second and third fingers from one gloved hand into the vaginal canal and **palpates** (feels) the cervix. By doing this, the physician can determine if there is any tenderness when the cervix is touched. Then, while the fingers remain in the vaginal canal, the physician may use his or her other hand to press in on the left and right lower abdominal areas. This technique can provide the examiner with valuable information. In non-obese patients, the physician can palpate the ovaries during a bimanual examination. Swelling or tenderness can then be assessed. Additionally, the physician may be able to identify the presence

(*continued on page 28*)

## GEORGE PAPANICOLAOU AND THE PAP SMEAR

George Papanicolaou was born in Kymi, Greece, in 1883. In 1898, he entered the University of Athens and with his physician father's guidance and encouragement, eventually attended medical school at the university and graduated in 1904. His first position as a physician, after graduation, involved caring for lepers in a leper colony in his hometown. Despite his father's suggestion to join the military as a physician and spend his career there, Papanicolaou decided to pursue a career in scientific research. To achieve that goal, Papanicolaou moved to Germany, where he earned his Ph.D. at the Institute of Munich in 1910. In 1914, he obtained a position in the Department of Anatomy at New York's Cornell Medical School and moved to the United States with his wife.

Papanicolaou began studying the cells from the lining of the vagina and the cervix, and through his work he was able to identify abnormal cells, specifically cancer cells. In 1928, he published the results of his endeavors entitled, "New Cancer Diagnosis." Papanicolaou then began collaborating with a gynecological pathologist, Dr. Herbert Taut. Together, they performed research that would confirm the potential for a test to reliably and accurately predict and diagnose cancer and early precancerous cells in the cervix. Their work was published in 1943, and the test was coined the *Pap smear*. While Papanicolaou could not predict it at the time, this early work would lead to a standard test performed on all women in their doctor's offices to identify the presence of cervical cancer. Nor could he ever have imagined that the adoption of this simple test, the Pap smear, would be part of the routine gynecologic examination for women that would lead to a great reduction in deaths from cervical cancer worldwide.

Dr. Papanicoloau received many honors and awards in his later life for his pioneering work in the early detection of cervical cancer in women. He died in 1962 and is buried in New Jersey.

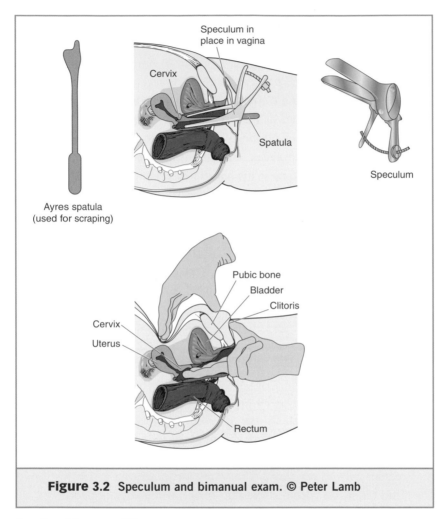

**Figure 3.2** Speculum and bimanual exam. © Peter Lamb

(*continued from page 26*)

of an ovarian abscess (pus collection) or an abscess adjacent to the ovaries in the adnexa.

## DIAGNOSIS

PID may cause a variety of clinical symptoms or no symptoms at all. For the physician or other healthcare provider caring for female patients, PID should always be considered a possible diagnosis when a woman who is sexually active complains of lower abdominal pain. Physicians are taught to look for abnormalities during the physical examination that may give further credence to the diagnosis of PID. Specifically, there are three clinical examination findings that should be present in a patient with PID. First, there is the finding of lower abdominal tenderness. This means that when the examiner presses in on the lower abdomen with his or her hands, the woman notes that the area is tender or painful. Second is the finding of cervical motion tenderness. If the patient notes pain during the bimanual examination, she is said to have cervical motion tenderness. The third physical examination finding that is common in women with PID is adnexal tenderness. Adnexal tenderness is identified when the woman feels pain while her left or right ovary is palpated during the bimanual examination. The presence of these three clinical examination findings in a sexually active woman should always lead to the presumptive diagnosis of PID.

There are several other clinical examination findings or laboratory data that can also help a healthcare provider make the diagnosis of PID, but they are not always present in every patient with PID and can often occur in patients without PID. Fever is one such examination finding. Similarly, an elevation in the number of circulating white blood cells (WBCs) often indicates an infection and can frequently occur in patients with PID. This finding, however, is not specific to the diagnosis of PID.

In the specific case of a woman with a suspected abscess of the ovary or fallopian tube, the diagnosis may be confirmed by **imaging** (taking pictures of) the pelvis. An **ultrasound** is one type of test that can provide images of the structures in the pelvis. In an ultrasound, a small **transducer** is pressed against the abdominal wall and bounces sound waves off the structures within the pelvis. A trained physician (usually a radiologist) can then interpret the pictures of the shadows made by these sound waves. The ultrasound test is a reliable way to identify the presence of an abscess in one of the upper genital tract structures. Another method of imaging a part of the body is the **computed tomography or CT scan**. This scan takes pictures of the body in a cross section as the patient lies flat on a table, using a camera in the walls of the CT machine that surrounds them. The images the CT scan collects can be looked at as sequential pictures of the body in a cross section starting from one point, say, the belly button (umbilicus), and ending at the level of the hip joints. An abscess of the ovary or fallopian tube is easily identified on a CT scan.

The most definitive way to make the diagnosis of PID is to actually look at the involved anatomic structures and confirm the presence of infection. This requires a surgical procedure called **laparoscopy**, in which a small, lighted tube with a camera at the tip is inserted through small incisions made in the abdominal wall. Once the laparoscope is inserted into the pelvic cavity, it can then be maneuvered to examine and send back pictures of the uterus, fallopian tubes, ovaries, and other anatomic structures in the pelvis. As this is quite invasive, and requires the woman to receive anesthesia, it is not routinely performed when the diagnosis of PID is being considered. The overwhelming majority of women with PID are diagnosed on the basis of their symptoms and the findings from their physical examinations.

Of course, the diagnosis of PID cannot be made by symptoms with the women who have no symptoms. In these situations, the diagnosis may only come to light if the physician identifies a suspicious physical examination finding during a routine physical examination or gynecological examination, or if he or she has performed screening tests for chlamydia or gonorrhea. Screening for asymptomatic gonorrhea or chlamydia infection is one of the most important tests a healthcare provider can perform in a sexually active woman. In fact, it is only by screening and diagnosing a gonorrhea or chlamydia infection before a woman develops symptoms of PID that physicians can actually prevent many of the long-term complications of PID. Screening is further discussed in Chapters 6 and 7.

## MANAGEMENT OF
## PELVIC INFLAMMATORY DISEASE

Several decisions must be made when managing a case of PID. First, the healthcare provider must decide whether or not the woman should be admitted to a hospital for care. Most women with PID have mild or moderate symptoms, and can be safely and effectively treated without being admitted to a hospital. Hospitalization is generally reserved for the small minority of women who are severely ill, with high fever, nausea and vomiting, or severe pain, or women who are unable to keep down anything taken by mouth. Additionally, any woman thought to have an abscess of the ovary or fallopian tubes should also be hospitalized, because abscesses must be drained.

The administration of antibiotics is the cornerstone of PID treatment. There are several effective antibiotics available for treating PID. The key to successful antibiotic therapy is in choosing the right antibiotic to effectively eradicate the bacteria that are believed to be the cause of the infection. In PID, this means choosing antibiotics that kill the bacteria responsible for gonorrhea and chlamydia. In women such as Jennifer who are mildly or moderately ill with PID and can be treated as outpatients (not being hospitalized), there are several antibiotic choices. Some antibiotic regimens can be given completely in oral-tablet form. Another treatment option is a single injection of an antibiotic into the muscle, followed by another antibiotic given as an oral tablet for the remainder of the course of therapy. When PID is severe enough to warrant hospitalization, intravenous antibiotics are usually given, at least in the first few days. Specifically, a small tube or catheter is inserted into a patient's vein (usually in the hand or forearm), and medicines and other fluids are delivered directly into the patient's veins and bloodstream. PID is always treated with a 14-day course of antibiotics, regardless of whether the antibiotic is given orally, injected into the muscle, administered by intravenous infusion, or in some combination of these methods.

Pain relief is another important part of the management of PID. Most often, the pain associated with PID responds to rest, antibiotic therapy, and simple over-the-counter pain medications available in pharmacies. In particular, ibuprofen (the medicine found in Motrin® and other preparations) is highly effective. Ibuprofen may also help decrease the inflammation or swelling of the tissues involved in the infection. Acetaminophen, the medicine found in Tylenol®, may also be helpful in pain relief. Rarely, women with PID may need strong, narcotic-type medications to relieve their pain. These are available only with a physician's prescription.

The optimal management of a woman with PID who is being treated as an outpatient is to have her return to the physician's office 72 hours after the start of therapy for a follow-up gynecological examination. Often, these women feel markedly better when they present for the follow-up examination, reporting that their fever has resolved, their pain is much improved, and that their nausea and vomiting have disappeared. On physical examination, the abdominal tenderness, cervical motion tenderness, and adnexal tenderness should all be diminished or resolved. In the rare instance where a woman is not better after 72 hours of therapy, she should be admitted to a hospital for further evaluation and intravenous antibiotics. In such cases, the possibility of an abscess in the ovary or fallopian tubes should be considered, and the woman should undergo either an ultrasound or CT scan imaging study.

If a woman is found to have a tubal or ovarian abscess, she is hospitalized and given intravenous antibiotics, as noted previously. If she does not respond to the antibiotic therapy within 72 hours, as exhibited by continued fevers or an increase in the size of the mass, then surgery to drain the abscess is usually required. The surgical procedure can be carried out in many ways. The patient may undergo a laparoscopy, as mentioned previously, in which the abscess is located and drained. Alternatively, the abscess may be identified and located by ultrasound or CT scan, a technique that enables the surgeon to insert a small drainage tube into the abscess. Another option is to have the abscess drained via a vaginal approach. A final possibility is that the patient may need to have an incision made into the pelvic cavity in order to find and drain the abscess.

The final component in the management of PID is to make sure that the patient's sexual partner(s) is identified, evaluated for sexually transmitted infections, and treated. The Centers for Disease Control and Prevention (CDC) recommends that all male sexual partners within the 60-day period preceding the diagnosis of PID should be preemptively treated for both gonorrhea and chlamydia infections. Patients must be told not to have sex with their partner until both they and their partner have completed all courses of antibiotic treatment.

# 4

# A Lifetime of Trouble: Complications of PID

## ACUTE COMPLICATIONS

PID can be associated with **acute** complications or complications that arise around the time of diagnosis, and **chronic** complications, those that may occur months or years after diagnosis and treatment. One of the most common acute complications—the formation of an abscess—has already been discussed. The management of abscesses depends upon the location, number, and size. A small abscess may respond to antibiotic therapy alone. Larger abscesses, or the presence of more than one abscess, are more likely to require some form of drainage (as described in Chapter 3).

Another acute complication of PID is the rupture of an ovarian or tubal abscess. When an abscess ruptures, it releases its contents (pus, which is made up of white blood cells and bacteria) into the pelvic and abdominal cavities. Infection may then spread throughout the pelvis and abdomen, and the patient can become gravely ill. Such an infection is called **peritonitis** because the peritoneum (the tissue lining the abdominal and pelvic cavities) becomes infected and inflamed. Patients with peritonitis experience intense abdominal pain and develop extreme sensitivity to touch in the abdominal region. Surgery is always required to treat peritonitis and to drain the infection that has spilled into the abdominal and pelvic cavities.

**Fitz-Hugh-Curtis syndrome** is a rare, acute complication of PID. In Fitz-Hugh-Curtis syndrome, the bacteria causing the PID (either *Chlamydia trachomatis* or *Neisseria gonorrhoeae)* are released into the peritoneal cavity and infect the capsule or tissue cover of the liver, known as **Glisson's capsule**. This type of infection is also known as a perihepatitis, because the area surrounding the liver is inflamed, but the liver itself is not. Women with Fitz-Hugh-Curtis syndrome experience moderate to severe right-sided upper abdominal pain with or without other symptoms like nausea or fever. As these women often do not have lower abdominal pain, the diagnosis of PID or any other STD is rarely considered. When examined, women with Fitz-Hugh-Curtis syndrome are found to have tenderness in their right upper abdomen. Most frequently, they are thought to have gallbladder disease—either acute inflammation of the gallbladder or gallstones with inflammation—or to have acute **hepatitis** (an inflammation of the liver itself). Tests that are performed to look for gallbladder disease or hepatitis, however, invariably return within the normal range. Fitz-Hugh-Curtis syndrome is ultimately a diagnosis that can be made by performing a laparoscopy to examine the abdominal and peritoneal cavities and their structures, including the liver and its capsule. When viewed this way, the capsule of the liver exhibits characteristic findings of inflammation along with adhesions, which are scar tissue that forms in response to the inflammation associated with the infection. In Fitz-Hugh-Curtis syndrome, these adhesions look like thick threads that are strung across the space between the capsule of the liver and the inner wall of the peritoneal cavity (and are called "violin-string" adhesions). A CT scan of the abdomen can sometimes show these adhesions and thus make the diagnosis of Fitz-Hugh-Curtis syndrome without the patient having to undergo an invasive laparoscopy. Fitz-Hugh-Curtis syndrome can be treated with antibiotics prescribed for PID, and patients usually have a resolution of their symptoms.

## CHRONIC COMPLICATIONS

The chronic complications of PID are varied and can be particularly troubling. The chronic complication most often

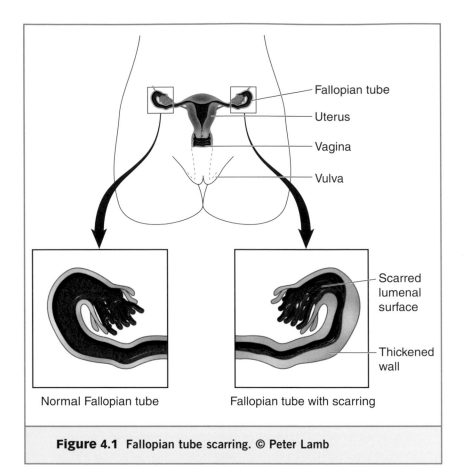

**Figure 4.1** Fallopian tube scarring. © Peter Lamb

discussed is infertility. There are many causes of infertility. In the United States, one in six couples have infertility problems, and 10 to 30 percent of them have infertility caused by damage to the fallopian tubes. In the case of a woman with a history of PID, infertility is most often caused by scarring of the fallopian tubes that occurs in the aftermath of the infection. The exact mechanisms that lead to tubal scarring and blockage are not well understood. It is believed, however, that the ongoing inflammation and swelling, especially in women with no symptoms, is at the center of the process. When the infecting bacteria ascend into the upper genital tract, and specifically into the fallopian tubes, they elicit an inflammatory response from the woman's immune system. White blood cells rush to the area to try to contain the infection. The white blood cells release many different compounds in an attempt to eradicate the bacteria. One effect of these compounds is the production of swelling and other signs of inflammation. This response from the immune system occurs regardless of whether the woman has symptoms of the infection or not. As one might imagine, if a woman has no symptoms of PID, this process could continue for months—possibly even years. Over time, this chronic inflammation leads to formation of scar tissue and narrowing of the fallopian tubes. Over time, the fallopian tubes become so narrow that eggs cannot travel down them and be deposited into the uterus. Without patent (open) fallopian tubes, a woman cannot become pregnant.

How likely is it for a woman who has had PID to become infertile? Research suggests that after one episode of PID, a woman has a 10 to 15 percent chance of being infertile. What is even more concerning, however, is that a woman who has had three or more episodes of PID has between a 50 and 80 percent chance of being infertile. It is believed that infertility may be a more common consequence of chlamydia than of gonorrhea. This is because chlamydia is less likely to cause symptoms and is thus a more common cause of silent PID, which allows the process of inflammation in the fallopian tubes and ovaries to continue, possibly for months or years, without being noticed. In the United States, rates of tubal infertility began to rise in the 1980s and 1990s, after an epidemic of gonorrhea and chlamydia in the 1970s and 1980s. Often, women in their late 20s or 30s will come to their gynecologist's office to find out why they cannot get pregnant, only to eventually be told it is most likely due to a previously undiagnosed chlamydia infection they may have had years earlier.

Another chronic complication of PID is **ectopic pregnancy**, a pregnancy in which the fertilized egg tries to implant

(*continued on page 40*)

## INFERTILITY

Infertility, the inability to conceive a child, affects one out of six couples in the United States. A couple is diagnosed as "infertile" when they have been unsuccessful in achieving pregnancy despite having unprotected sexual intercourse for

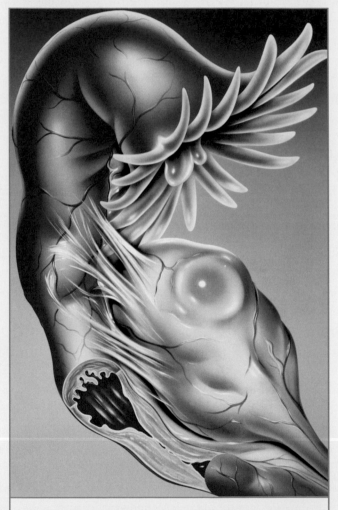

**Figure 4.2** Fallopian tube infertility. © John Bavosi/ Photo Researchers, Inc.

one year. When the female partner is unable to reproduce, the condition is referred to as female infertility. Female infertility contributes to approximately one-half of all infertility cases, while female infertility factors alone are responsible for one-third of infertile couples. Female infertility occurs when there is a problem with ovulation (the process whereby the ovary releases a viable egg for fertilization), there is damage to the fallopian tubes or uterus, or there is a problem with the cervix. Abnormal cervical mucus can cause infertility because it can prevent the sperm from reaching or penetrating the egg. The age of the woman is a big factor in determining fertility, because every woman is born with a fixed number of eggs. As the reproductive years pass and a woman ages, the number of viable eggs she has decreases dramatically. Women between the ages of 30 and 34 are 14 percent less fertile than women between the ages of 20 and 24. Women between the ages of 35 and 39 are 31 percent less fertile than women in their early 20s.

Problems with ovulation may be caused by a variety of factors, including:

1. An imbalance of female hormones
2. A tumor or cyst on the ovary
3. Eating disorders like anorexia or bulimia
4. Intense exercise that leads to a loss of body fat
5. Obesity
6. Alcohol or drug use
7. An extremely short menstrual cycle

The fallopian tubes or uterus can be damaged in several ways, including:

1. Pelvic inflammatory disease
2. Polyps or fibroid tumors of the uterus
3. Endometriosis (a build-up of retained uterine tissue

that can be deposited within the uterus or outside it in various parts of the pelvic or abdominal cavity)
4. Scar tissue from previous infections or surgeries
5. Certain birth defects
6. Exposure to certain drugs

A trained specialist diagnoses female infertility after thorough testing is performed. Such tests include screening for sexually transmitted diseases, laparoscopy, and special X-ray studies. Samples are often taken from urine, blood, and cervical mucus. Women evaluated for infertility are often asked to keep track of their daily temperature to identify exactly when they ovulate. On the days nearing ovulation, a woman's temperature rises, and thus a woman can often identify when ovulation takes place.

Female infertility can be treated, depending upon the cause. When common treatments are unsuccessful, a couple can consider in vitro fertilization to achieve pregnancy. In the *in vitro* fertilization process, an egg is taken from a woman and sperm is taken from the man, and the egg is fertilized in a laboratory. The fertilized egg is then placed into the uterus of the female to promote implantation to the uterine lining.

(*continued from page 37*)

itself someplace other than the lining of the uterus wall. Ectopic pregnancies can occur in the fallopian tubes, in the abdominal cavity, or can attach to other abdominal structures. No matter where the ectopic pregnancy tries to implant outside of the uterus, it cannot become a viable pregnancy. The fertilized egg causes symptoms as it begins to grow. A woman with an ectopic pregnancy eventually develops symptoms and ultimately requires surgical intervention. Ectopic pregnancies cause significant illness and in rare cases can lead to death. In

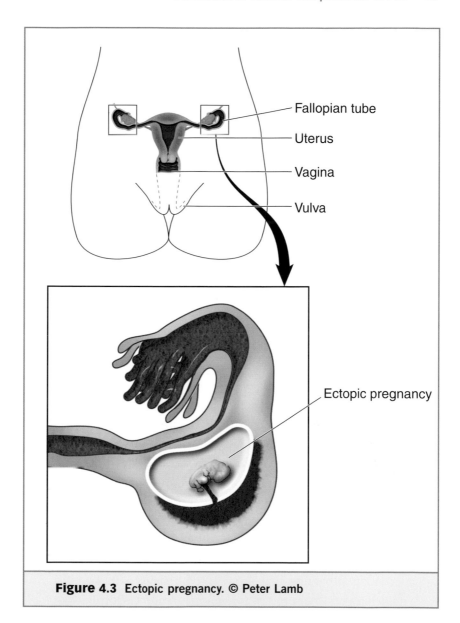

**Figure 4.3** Ectopic pregnancy. © Peter Lamb

the developing world in particular, there can be a long delay in the diagnosis of an ectopic pregnancy. As a result, the structure to which it has attached can become severely damaged, and in some women, this can lead to death. A woman with a history of PID has a higher risk of having an ectopic pregnancy. Some estimates suggest that the risk of having an ectopic pregnancy is eight times greater in a woman who becomes pregnant after having had PID.

The last chronic complication of PID is chronic pelvic pain. How common this problem is after PID has not been well studied, so there are no reliable estimates about its frequency. Many women suffer from chronic pain in the lower abdomen after they have been successfully treated for PID. The pain is usually due to scar tissue that has formed after the swelling and inflammation that occurred during the acute infection. For many women, the pain can be difficult to manage; often, pain medications are not entirely effective. Most of these women eventually have surgery to alleviate their chronic pain; a **hysterectomy** (removal of the uterus) with or without an **oophorectomy** (removal of the ovaries) is usually performed.

What is perhaps most troubling about the chronic complications of PID is that they are not prevented by treating the acute episode of PID with antibiotics. This aspect of PID management has been studied, and it has been shown that antibiotic therapy for women with PID cannot decrease the subsequent risk of developing infertility, an ectopic pregnancy, or chronic pelvic pain. The only way these complications of PID can be truly prevented is by preventing gonorrhea and chlamydia entirely, through behavioral changes in the population, or by finding and treating gonorrhea and chlamydia in women before they develop signs and symptoms of an upper genital tract infection. As the next two chapters describe, screening programs that provide physicians with specific guidelines on whom to test for gonorrhea and chlamydia—as well as when and how often—have been developed by the CDC.

# 5

# Bacterial Cause of PID: Gonorrhea

## A BRIEF HISTORY OF AN ANCIENT DISEASE

Gonorrhea is a disease that has been recognized for thousands of years. References to the urethritis it commonly causes in men can be found in the Old Testament of the Bible, in ancient Chinese writings, and other historic works. In A.D. 130, the Greek scientist and physician Galen coined the term *gonorrhea*, which means "flow of seed." This term refers to the fact that the primary symptom of urethritis in men, the urethral discharge, can look like semen. The bacterium *Neisseria gonorrhoeae* was first identified by Albert Neisser in 1879 and grown in culture in 1882 by Leistikow and Löffler. Until the 1930s, there was no effective therapy available for treatment of gonorrhea; most people with gonorrhea lived with their infection until it ran its course, which could be months, and were then left with chronic problems such as scar tissue in the urethra, which limited the ability to urinate. With the advent of penicillin in the 1940s, treatment and cure of gonorrhea became possible, and many of these chronic complications disappeared.

The bacterium that causes gonorrhea, *Neisseria gonorrhoeae*, has over the last 60 years become resistant to penicillin and other antibiotics used to treat it. The organism's ability to develop resistance to the antibiotics used to treat it has made *Neisseria gonorrhoeae* a bacterium of great interest to microbiologists and other scientists who study bacteria. Despite highly effective antibiotics, gonorrhea remains one of the most commonly reported infectious diseases in the United States today. The reasons for this are complex, and will be discussed below.

(*continued on page 46*)

## *NEISSERIA GONORRHOEAE* AND RESISTANCE TO ANTIBIOTICS

*Neisseria gonorrhoeae* is an interesting bacterium to many microbiologists, researchers, and physicians throughout the world, not only for the varied kinds of disease it can cause in humans, but because of its uncanny ability to develop resistance to the antibiotics that are usually used to treat it. While many bacteria are naturally resistant to the killing effects of certain antibiotics, *N. gonorrhoeae* is one that, over the past 60 years, has evolved and developed mutations that have allowed it to survive and become immune to treatment with certain types of antibiotics.

The history of this evolution began in the mid-1940s. Soon after World War II, a new "wonder drug" called penicillin became widely available in the United States. One of the benefits that had been discovered by military doctors was that penicillin could effectively cure gonorrhea and syphilis infections in their troops. The advent of penicillin led to dramatic decreases in the number of new gonococcal infections and syphilis cases in the Unites States. Within 10 years of using penicillin for treatment of gonorrhea infections, however, many doctors noticed that the originally recommended dose was no longer working effectively. Microbiologists soon discovered why. *N. gonorrhoeae* had developed a mutation in its cell wall that allowed it to become somewhat impervious to the penicillin compound. By giving higher doses, this mutation could be overcome and enough penicillin could penetrate into the bacterium to kill it and cure infection. Thus, from the late 1940s until the early 1970s, the dose of penicillin required to cure a case of gonorrhea rose continually. This phenomenon has never been seen with syphilis, which is caused by the bacterium *Treponema pallidum*.

In the late 1960s, *N. gonorrhoeae* picked up a special piece of DNA called a "plasmid" from another species of bacteria. This plasmid contained encoded genes to make an enzyme that destroyed the penicillin compound and rendered any dose of penicillin ineffective for treating gonorrhea infections. Because of the increasing incidence of penicillin resistance in *N. gonorrhoeae*, penicillin is no longer used as the antibiotic of choice for the initial treatment of an infection for treatment of gonorrhea. In the 1970s, doctors began using antibiotics called tetracyclines as their first-line antibiotic to treat gonorrhea infections. However, this bacterium again developed resistance to the killing effects of the tetracyclines. In the 1980s, certain antibiotics in the class of drugs called the cephalosporins became the drug of choice; however, the drug usually had to be delivered through a painful injection into a muscle. In the 1990s, a new class of antibiotics called fluoroquinolones was found to be very effective in treating gonorrhea infections, and they could be given as one oral tablet. For this reason, fluoroquinolones rapidly became the preferred antibiotics for treating gonorrhea.

Not surprisingly to those who have studied the history of *N. gonorrhoeae* and its resistance to antibiotics, in the late 1990s and the early part of the 21st century, it was identified that some patients with gonorrhea infections were not being cured by a fluoroquinolone treatment. *N. gonorrhoeae* had developed yet another new mutation that allowed it to evade the killing activity of the fluoroquinolones. What will *N. gonorrhoeae* do next? One can be sure that the ability of this organism to adapt and evolve despite the presence of antibiotics will continue to cause problems for physicians who treat patients with gonorrhea infections and fascinate microbiologists who study bacteria.

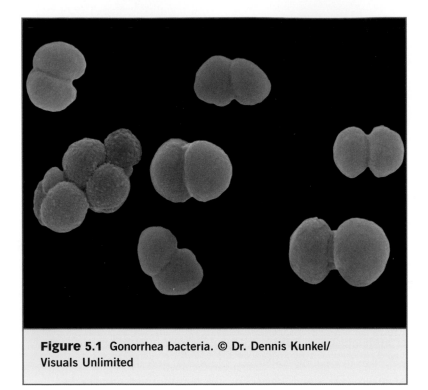

**Figure 5.1** Gonorrhea bacteria. © Dr. Dennis Kunkel/ Visuals Unlimited

(*continued from page 43*)

## MICROBIOLOGY OF *NEISSERIA GONORRHOEAE*

All bacteria can be classified two ways: by their shape when viewed under a microscope and by the way their cell walls take up a Gram stain. A bacterium that is round is called a **coccus** (plural, **cocci**); a bacterium that has an elongated, tubular shape is called a **rod**. The Gram stain, developed by Danish bacteriologist Christian Gram, is a technique that distinguishes between two groups of bacteria by the identification of differences in the structure of their cell walls. **Gram-positive bacteria** stain purple, whereas **Gram-negative bacteria** stain red. *Neisseria gonorrhoeae* is a Gram-negative coccus that grows in pairs (diplococci), with the sides that touch being slightly flattened. The diplococci are often described as resembling two kidney beans next to one another. *Neisseria gonorrhoeae* will grow in the laboratory under

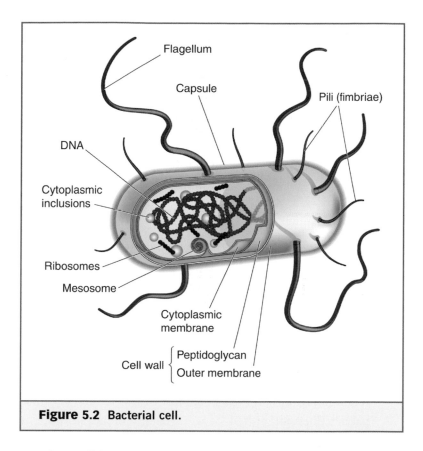

Flagellum

Capsule

Pili (fimbriae)

DNA

Cytoplasmic
inclusions

Ribosomes

Mesosome

Cytoplasmic
membrane

Cell wall { Peptidoglycan
             Outer membrane

**Figure 5.2**  Bacterial cell.

specific conditions, including appropriate temperature, the right incubator, and the presence of nutrients to enhance its growth.

Several structures in the bacterial cell wall, or envelope, of *Neisseria gonorrhoeae* allow the bacterium to infect human host cells. These structures include **pili** (singular, **pilus**), the outer membrane proteins, and a component of the cell membrane called lipooligosaccharide. The pili extend out from the surface of the bacterial cell wall like long tentacles, enabling the bacteria to efficiently attach themselves to the human host cells. Once the bacteria are attached, they need to be taken up into the host cell to spread to other cells within the host. The outer membrane proteins promote these activities and are also able to evade some of the human immune system's responses, thus making *Neisseria gonorrhoeae* very capable of causing disease. The lipooligosaccharide on the cell surface also contributes to the ability of the organism to invade host cells, causing them to become abnormal and die.

## TRANSMISSION OF GONORRHEA

*Neisseria gonorrhoeae* is almost always transmitted through unprotected sexual intercourse with an infected partner. Exceptions include pregnant women with gonorrhea who can transmit the infection to their newborns during passage of the newborn through an infected birth canal. Individuals with gonorrhea can also, under certain circumstances and due to poor hygiene, spread their infection to another body site via their hands. Specifically, a man with gonococcal urethritis may touch the discharge and then touch his eye, leading to spread of the infection to the conjunctiva, or lining of the eyelid.

If a woman has unprotected vaginal intercourse with a man with gonorrhea, her chance of acquiring infection is approximately 50 to 70 percent with each episode of unprotected intercourse. If the woman has gonorrhea and her male partner does not, his risk of acquiring gonorrhea from her is approximately 20 percent with each unprotected vaginal intercourse. Transmission by anal intercourse occurs, but exact risk percentages are not known. Gonorrhea may also be transmitted through oral sex; specifically, to the male recipient of oral intercourse. The organism can reside in the throat and cause infection there, and can then be transmitted to the male urethra during oral intercourse. In most situations, gonorrhea is transmitted by an individual who has minimal or no symptoms.

## INCIDENCE OF, AND RISK FACTORS FOR, GONORRHEA

In the United States, gonorrhea is a **reportable disease**, that is, a disease that must be reported to public health authorities

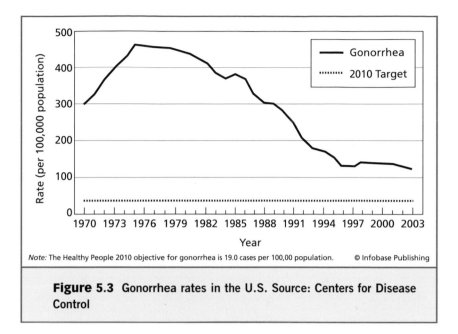

Note: The Healthy People 2010 objective for gonorrhea is 19.0 cases per 100,00 population.    © Infobase Publishing

**Figure 5.3** Gonorrhea rates in the U.S. Source: Centers for Disease Control

when it is diagnosed. Whenever a laboratory receives a specimen that tests positive for *Neisseria gonorrhoeae*, the laboratory is required by law to report the infection to the local health department. Local health departments then collect this data and report it to the state health departments, who in turn report it to the CDC. The number of reported cases of gonorrhea each year is estimated to be about half of what truly occurs across the United States. There are many reasons why not all cases of gonorrhea are reported or counted. Some patients are treated for the infection but never tested to confirm the presence of gonorrhea. Other patients may be tested but have a negative test result for various reasons, including failure to collect the specimen properly, failure to get the specimen to the laboratory in a timely manner, or practical limitations of the test to detect *Neisseria gonorrhoeae*.

In the United States, the highest number of cases of gonorrhea occurred in the 1970s. With the implementation of several public health interventions, the incidence of gonorrhea

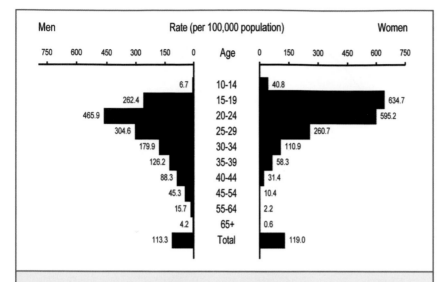

**Figure 5.4** Gonorrhea rates by age. Source: Centers for Disease Control

declined from the late 1970s through the mid-1990s. From 1998 through 2002, total case numbers were relatively stable, but in 2002 the numbers began to rise again.

Gonorrhea in the United States is most often seen in individuals between the ages of 15 and 24. Rates are highest in 15- to 19-year-old women and 20 to 24-year-old men. Gonorrhea is therefore most commonly a disease of adolescents and young adults. In women between the ages of 15 and 19, the number of gonorrhea cases is five to six times higher than the overall national average. This is a very important statistic. It means that large numbers of teens and young adults are having unprotected sexual intercourse, which places them at risk for other STDs, including HIV infection (which can lead to acquired immunodeficiency syndrome, or AIDS). When cases of gonorrhea are broken down by race and ethnicity, African Americans have the highest rates of gonorrhea infection in the United States. Race is a marker for other risk factors, and not in and of itself something that enhances susceptibility to

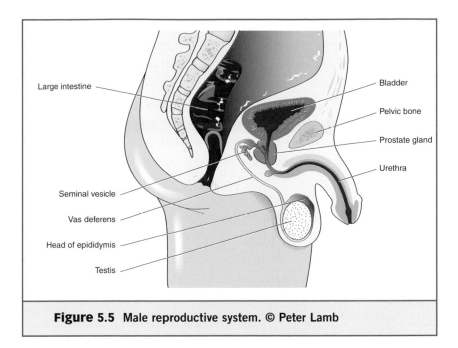

Large intestine

Seminal vesicle

Vas deferens

Head of epididymis

Testis

Bladder

Pelvic bone

Prostate gland

Urethra

**Figure 5.5** Male reproductive system. © Peter Lamb

infection. Other risk factors for gonorrhea infection in the United States include residence in the southeastern part of the country, low socioeconomic status, lack of formal education, and use of illicit drugs.

## CLINICAL ILLNESSES CAUSED BY *NEISSERIA GONORRHOEAE*

As outlined in Chapter 2, gonorrhea causes different types of illness depending on which body site it is inoculated into. In men, the most common type of infection is urethritis, which is infection and inflammation of the cells lining the urethra (the urinary canal of the penis). Men with urethritis experience burning when they urinate and usually have a discharge from the urethra that can be white, yellow, or green and of variable amount. Approximately 90 percent of men with urethral gonorrhea infection develop these symptoms; the remaining 10 percent have no symptoms. Without treatment, gonococcal urethritis can spontaneously resolve over many weeks or a few months. Rarely, a man—especially one who has had repeat infections—can eventually develop something called a **stricture**, which is scar tissue in the urethra. The stricture can cause difficulty with urination and ejaculation. Also, in unusual circumstances, gonorrhea may travel from the urethra to the epididymis, the gland that lies above the testicles in the scrotum, and cause epididymitis (swelling and infection of the epididymis). A man with epididymitis experiences painful swelling and redness of the involved area of the scrotum. He may or may not have symptoms of urethritis or presence of penile discharge at the time.

The cervix is made up of two different types of cells: the **ectocervix**, or outermost portion of the cervix, has squamous epithelial cells called ectocervical cells; the **endocervix**, or inner portion of the cervix, consists of columnar (column-shaped) epithelial cells called endocervical cells. The first site of gonococcal infection in women is the cervix, specifically, the endocervical cells. Sometimes, the urethra can also be infected in women. The cells that make up the lining of the vagina are not susceptible to infection with *Neisseria gonorrhoeae,* so gonorrhea does not cause vaginitis (inflammation of the vagina). Gonorrhea infection of the cervix (cervicitis) occurs without symptoms in approximately 50 percent of women. Women with symptoms of cervicitis experience vaginal discharge and may also have bleeding not at the time of menstruation and burning or pain with urination. On examination, the cervix can appear entirely normal or it can show evidence of swelling, redness, easy bleeding when swabbed, or the presence of a discharge coming out of the opening (os) of the cervix. The symptoms of women with gonorrhea of the upper genital tract, or PID, have been described in detail in Chapters 1 and 3.

Rectal infection with *Neisseria gonorrhoeae* can occur in both men and women. In women, rectal infection is usually the result of the following sequence of events: (1) the organism is present in cervical and vaginal secretions, (2) these secretions contaminate the area between the vaginal opening and the anus, (3) the organism travels through the anus to the rectum, and (4) the bacteria infect the cells in the lining of the rectal wall. Alternatively, *Neisseria gonorrhoeae* may be inoculated into the rectum during receptive anal intercourse, which is the predominant route of transmission of rectal gonorrhea in men. In both women and men, the infection is often without symptoms; however, men tend to have symptoms more often than women. Symptoms of rectal gonorrhea can include anal itching, pain with bowel movements, discharge from the rectum, or rectal bleeding. Such symptoms are called proctitis and can also be caused by *Chlamydia trachomatis* infection, as well as herpes virus infection, syphilis, and other STDs.

Gonorrhea can cause an infection in the throat, when inoculated into the site during oral sex. Pharyngeal gonorrhea is almost always without symptoms. When *Neisseria* is inoculated into the eye, it causes conjunctivitis (swelling and inflammation of the conjunctivae, the tissue lining the eyelid). Infection of the eye is always symptomatic and can rapidly become a severe infection that progresses to an **ulcer** (a deep sore) of the cornea in some patients. As noted above, most adults with gonococcal conjunctivitis acquired the infection through self-inoculation from their hands.

## DIAGNOSIS OF GONORRHEA

The diagnosis of gonorrhea is made when a laboratory test detects the presence of *Neisseria gonorrhoeae* in a clinical specimen taken from the patient. In men with urethritis, the specimen may be either a swab of the urethra, urethral discharge, or urine. In women, it may be a swab of the endocervix or urine. There are two different types of testing for the presence of *Neisseria gonorrhoeae* in a clinical specimen. First, there is a culture. With a bacterial culture, the specimen is inoculated onto an agar plate that has the right nutrients and other compounds to encourage the growth of *Neisseria gonorrhoeae.* If the organism will grow, it will do so after 24 to 48 hours. There are several limitations to bacterial culture when used to diagnose gonorrhea. The organism can die if the specimen is not inoculated onto the agar plate in a timely fashion. Also, the agar plate must be placed into an incubator quickly to allow the organism to remain viable. Finally, even with ideal culture techniques and conditions, in some instances the specimen collection was not adequate and the culture fails to grow.

One positive aspect of culture is that the organism is available for testing of its resistance or susceptibility to different antibiotics. Although antibiotic susceptibility and resistance is not routinely tested for *Neisseria gonorrhoeae* in most laboratories, it is something that is monitored nationally by the CDC. The ability of *Neisseria gonorrhoeae* to develop resistance to the antibiotics most commonly prescribed to treat it has been noted for 40 years. This continues to be one of the many challenges doctors and public health officials face in trying to limit, control, and eradicate the infection.

The other laboratory technique that is now commonly used to diagnose gonorrhea does not have the limitations of bacterial culturing. These tests are called **nucleic acid amplification tests**, or NAATs. There are several of these tests available in the United States, all of them relying upon the same general laboratory principle or technique. NAATs search the clinical specimen for small parts of the DNA of *Neisseria gonorrhoeae* within the specimen and then amplify these DNA sequences. The major drawback to these testing techniques is that the bacteria are not available for additional antibiotic susceptibility tests.

# 6

# Bacterial Cause of PID: Chlamydia

## A BRIEF HISTORY OF CHLAMYDIA

*Chlamydia trachomatis* was only identified as a bacterium and as a cause of a variety of infections in 1963. The name chlamydia is derived from the Greek word "chlamys," meaning "cloak draped across the shoulder." This is because the bacterium is draped around the infected cell's nucleus.

*Chlamydia trachomatis* is divided into 15 different **serovars** or types. Serovars A, B, Ba, and C cause infection of the eye called **ocular trachoma**. Ocular trachoma is the most common cause of preventable blindness globally and accounts for between seven million and nine million people with vision loss worldwide. Ocular trachoma is an ancient disease (though the cause was unknown in ancient times), but is now only seen in the developing world. This type of chlamydia infection is not sexually transmitted, but rather is transmitted by hand-to-eye contact in children, or through a **fly vector**, or carrier of disease. Serovars D, E, F, G, H, I, J, and K cause urogenital tract infections and a milder form of eye infection (conjunctivitis) that does not lead to blindness. These serovars are responsible for the STD that many people in the United States refer to as simply "chlamydia."

Serovars L1, L2, and L3, like serovars D through K, are also sexually transmitted, but cause a different clinical disease called **lymphogranuloma venereum** (LGV). The serovars that cause LGV are common in Africa, India, South America, and Southeast Asia. LGV is very rare in the United States and other industrialized countries in the Northern Hemisphere. LGV causes a unique clinical disease that centers on the lymph nodes.

When the *Chlamydia trachomatis* L1, L2, or L3 serovar is acquired via the urethral site (usually in men, sometimes in women), the lymph nodes in the groin become infected, swollen, and very painful. In some patients, they drain pus. Patients generally have fevers and feel like they have the flu. In some cases, the lymph nodes can drain fluid for months or even years. Without treatment, the lymph nodes become scarred and nonfunctional, and the patient has considerable swelling on the infected side, which can include the leg. When *Chlamydia*

## SILENT EPIDEMICS OF SEXUALLY TRANSMITTED DISEASES

Each year, three million new cases of chlamydia infections are diagnosed in the United States. However, this is a gross underestimate of the actual numbers, which could be close to double that amount. Chlamydia is often called the silent epidemic, because so many infected people are not aware of their illness. Up to 75 percent of women and 50 percent of men who are infected have absolutely no symptoms. When a sexually transmitted disease (STD) causes no symptoms, it can be easily spread from one person to another because partners do not seek out care and are therefore never treated. The ongoing spread of infection in a community or population is often called an epidemic.

While it is usually chlamydia that receives the most attention when researchers and physicians talk about a silent STD epidemic, many other STDs similarly go undiagnosed, and the untreated individuals with infection become a reservoir for spread of the disease. Gonorrhea can be present without any symptoms, particularly in women, where up to 50 percent of women with lower genital tract infection may be completely symptom-free. Syphilis can often cause only minor symptoms that a patient can easily ignore. The first stage of syphilis infection, particularly in women, usually has no symptoms and goes undiagnosed. Many patients, both men and women, can easily pass through the second stage of infection without coming to the attention of a healthcare provider. Genital herpes infections are caused by a herpes virus; they are most often transmitted when the infected partner looks and feels fine but is actually shedding the herpes virus in his or her genital secretions. Many individuals who have been infected with the herpes virus have never had a genital herpes outbreak and are thus "silently" infected. Human papillomaviruses (HPV) are sexually transmitted diseases that can cause genital warts and some cancers in both men and women. The HPV types that cause cervical cancer trigger absolutely no symptoms and are thus also silent. The changes caused by the HPV infection in the cells of the woman's cervix are only detected through routine screening for cervical cancer with the Pap smear. Finally, the STD trichomoniasis, which is caused by a parasite called *Trichomonas vaginalis,* is almost always without symptoms in men and causes no symptoms in 50 percent of women who are infected. Thus all STDs, and not just chlamydia, contribute to the silent epidemic of infections that eventually cause so much trouble for millions of individuals.

*trachomatis* L1, L2, or L3 is acquired through the rectal mucosa, the patient may develop proctitis or proctocolitis, where the infection extends from the rectum into the colon. This type of LGV is most commonly seen in homosexual men. Treatment of LGV is different from that for infection with serovars D-K.

## MICROBIOLOGY OF *CHLAMYDIA TRACHOMATIS*

*Chlamydia trachomatis* can only survive by being taken up into the host cells. Once it is inside the host cells, it can then

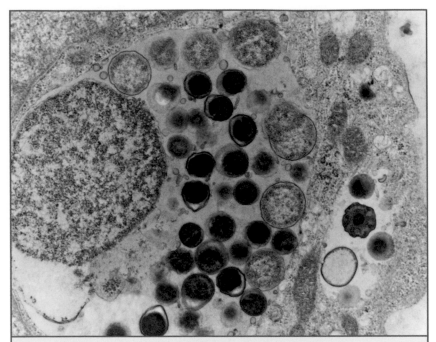

**Figure 6.1** Cell infected with chlamydia. © Dr. Fred Hossler/Visuals Unlimited

reproduce and complete its life cycle. There are two phases in the life cycle of the bacterium. In the first phase, the bacterium is called an **elementary body**. In this form, *Chlamydia trachomatis* survives outside the host cell, is transmissible, and attaches to and binds with the surface of another host cell. The elementary body is the infectious form of chlamydia bacterium. Once the elementary body has attached to the surface of the host's cell (the endocervical cell in women or the urethral epithelial cell in men), the host cell allows it to enter, or be absorbed into, the inside of the cell. Once the elementary body is inside the host cell, it converts itself into the second form of the *Chlamydia trachomatis* bacterium and enters into the second phase of the life cycle. This intracellular form is called the **reticulate body**, and in this form is capable of reproducing within the host cell. Using the host cell's proteins, the reticulate body may replicate into anywhere from 100 to 1,000 new infectious elementary bodies, which are then released into the host to infect adjacent cells.

Although there is a response from the host's immune system, it is not very effective and does not protect the host from future infections. Having had one infection with chlamydia does not confer any protection against further infection in the host. In fact, patients can have many infections over a lifetime and be infected with more than one *Chlamydia trachomatis* serovar at the same time.

## TRANSMISSION OF *CHLAMYDIA TRACHOMATIS* SEROVARS D-K

Unlike with gonorrhea, the risk of acquiring chlamydia infection with a single episode of unprotected sexual intercourse is unknown. It appears to be lower than with gonorrhea, and some experts have suggested that the risk may be between 30 and 35 percent. *Chlamydia trachomatis* is transmitted through vaginal intercourse, rectal intercourse, and probably least efficiently through oral sex, though this is not well studied. Most infected individuals are without symptoms and thus unknowingly spread the infection to their sexual partners.

## INCIDENCE OF, AND RISK FACTORS FOR, *CHLAMYDIA TRACHOMATIS* SEROVARS D-K

In the United States, there are approximately four million new cases of *Chlamydia trachomatis* infection each year. For the past several years, it has been the most commonly reported infectious disease to the CDC. Approximately 25 percent of these total infections occur in adolescents between the ages of 15 and 19 in the United States. The strongest risk factor for chlamydia infection in a woman is having a male partner with either gonorrhea or symptoms of urethritis. Gonorrhea is a risk factor for chlamydia infection, as the two bacteria often coinfect the same

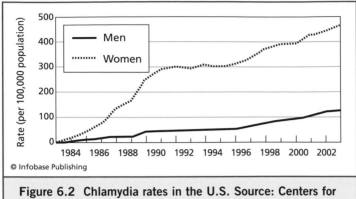

**Figure 6.2   Chlamydia rates in the U.S. Source: Centers for Disease Control**

person. In the United States, those that are most likely to acquire chlamydia are between the ages of 15 and 25, single, and have multiple sexual partners (defined as two or more partners in the preceding three months). Higher rates of chlamydia infection are seen in the southeastern portion of the country, as with gonorrhea. African Americans are also at a higher risk for infection. Use of oral contraceptives (birth control pills) has been found to be a risk factor for chlamydia. It is not known, however, if this is because using birth control pills makes young women less likely to use condoms or because the hormones in the birth control pills increase the woman's susceptibility to chlamydia infection. Being an adolescent is the strongest risk factor for chlamydia infection in sexually active women in the United States. Youth is also associated with being at high risk for repeat infections, for PID, and for ectopic pregnancy and infertility.

Approximately 50 percent of men and 70 percent of women with chlamydia have minimal or no symptoms. The asymptomatic nature of chlamydia infections is a critical point to comprehend in order to fully understand the disease. The implications are greatest when one thinks of how many diseases are identified in patients. Most diseases are diagnosed after the patient presents to his or her doctor with a symptom. If doctors only looked for chlamydia infection in patients with symptoms, the overwhelming majority of chlamydia infections in the United States would go undiagnosed and thus untreated. To identify the majority of patients infected with *Chlamydia trachomatis*, physicians must thus look for, or screen, patients without any symptoms. Screening recommendations have been made by the CDC and are based on what is currently known to be the most likely risk factors for chlamydia infection. More on the importance of screening as the cornerstone of chlamydia and PID prevention programs can be found in Chapter 7.

## CLINICAL ILLNESSES CAUSED BY *CHLAMYDIA TRACHOMATIS* SEROVARS D-K

Men with chlamydia can develop urethritis or epididymitis, just as with gonorrhea. The symptoms and physical examination findings are very similar to gonorrhea; however, the urethral discharge tends to be clear, white, or gray, and is less likely to look like pus, as it does in gonorrhea. Additionally, some men with chlamydia urethritis may only have a very small amount of penile discharge that occurs only in the morning and may not report it as something unusual unless asked specifically about it.

Women with chlamydia infection develop cervicitis. Usually the cervicitis is without symptoms, but when symptoms are present, they can be varied and include vaginal discharge, bleeding, or pain during intercourse. Some women may have what appears to be a common urinary tract infection, with burning and pain during urination and frequent urination, but is in fact chlamydia urethritis, also known as "acute urethral syndrome."

Overall, it has been estimated that eight percent of women with chlamydia cervicitis develop an upper genital tract infection (PID). The likelihood of progression of chlamydia infection to the upper genital tract varies by population group, however. PID encompasses **endometritis** (inflammation of the walls of the uterus), **salpingitis** (inflammation of the fallopian tubes), or **peritonitis** (inflammation of the abdominal cavity), and can involve any or all of these conditions.

When a pregnant woman has undiagnosed chlamydia at the time of delivery, she may transmit the infection to her newborn during the baby's passage through the infected birth canal. Newborns can then develop two different types of chlamydia. First, they may develop conjunctivitis. Estimates suggest that 22 to 44 percent of infants born to infected mothers have conjunctivitis, which usually manifests within two weeks of birth. The baby first has a watery discharge from the eye. Next, the tissues around the eye become red and swollen. Finally, thick, yellow, pus-like discharge develops.

Infant pneumonia is the second type of infection a newborn may develop as a result of infection during delivery. An estimated 11 to 20 percent of infants born to infected mothers have pneumonia. Most infants develop symptoms in the first eight weeks of life. Fever is usually not a prominent complaint, but a cough is always present. Chest X-rays show involvement of both lungs. With either type of infant chlamydia infection, antibiotic treatment rapidly improves an infant's symptoms.

## DIAGNOSIS OF *CHLAMYDIA TRACHOMATIS* INFECTION

Because *Chlamydia trachomatis* can only grow and reproduce when it is inside living cells, it cannot be grown in an agar plate culture like *Neisseria gonorrhoeae* or other bacteria. Instead, to grow *Chlamydia trachomatis* in culture, the specimen must be inoculated into living cells in a laboratory. These cells are then incubated and studied to determine if changes occur that are consistent with the presence of *Chlamydia trachomatis*. There are many technical limitations to cell culture that affect the likelihood of having a positive culture. Because of this, culture of *Chlamydia trachomatis* is never used as a routine diagnostic test when a patient is being screened for possible chlamydia infection. Instead, nonculture diagnostic tests are used in the United States. One group of nonculture tests can help diagnose the presence of *Chlamydia trachomatis* by searching the specimen for proteins, RNA (ribonucleic acid), or other compounds unique to the bacterium. There must be 1,000 to 10,000 elementary bodies in the specimen for these tests to detect the presence of *Chlamydia trachomatis* and read positive. If there are fewer than 1,000 elementary bodies, the tests will be negative and a patient's infection may be missed. Clinical specimens required for these tests are endocervical swabs from women or urethral swabs from men. To obtain these specimens, the patient must undergo a relatively noninvasive procedure for collection of the specimen; women must have a pelvic examination and men must have a small cotton swab inserted into their urethra. Both procedures can be uncomfortable.

Nucleic acid amplification tests (NAATs; see Chapter 5) use probes to find pieces of chlamydial DNA (deoxyribonucleic acid) or RNA in clinical specimens and then amplify or reproduce these pieces to make the diagnosis. NAATs can detect as few as one to ten elementary bodies in clinical specimens. Because these tests are so sensitive, urine can be used as an alternative clinical specimen from both men and women who require screening for chlamydia infection. NAATs have made truly noninvasive testing for chlamydial infection possible for the first time. They have been used to develop community-based screening programs at high schools, juvenile detention centers, prisons, and military recruiting facilities. Adolescents and young adults are more willing to participate in such screening programs when they require only urine samples and not more uncomfortable, invasive procedures.

# 7

# Prevention of PID and Its Complications

## WHAT CAN BE DONE?

Prevention of PID and its complications can only be achieved by preventing gonorrhea and chlamydia entirely or by identifying them quickly and effectively and eradicating them with reliable antibiotic therapy before they ascend into the upper genital tract. Primary prevention of gonorrhea and chlamydia can only occur with behavioral changes in the population, including delaying sexual activity among adolescents and use of condoms during intercourse. Another important component of PID prevention is making sure the patient and the patient's sexual partners are all effectively treated to stop the spread of the STDs. A third component is instituting regular screening in patients who are most at risk of having chlamydia or gonorrhea infection. Future prospects include vaccine development for both *Neisseria gonorrhoeae* and *Chlamydia trachomatis*, bacteria that have thus far eluded research efforts to develop an effective vaccine. Realistically, prevention of these infections through immunization is likely decades away from being realized.

## BEHAVIORAL PREVENTION STRATEGIES

To prevent gonorrhea and chlamydia from spreading, behavioral changes in at-risk populations must be encouraged and taught. Primary prevention strategies include delaying sexual activity, as adolescents are at the highest risk of acquiring one of these STDs and of spreading them to their partners. Limiting the number of sexual partners should also be promoted as a prevention strategy in at-risk populations. Another behavioral message that must be shared is the consistent and correct use of latex condoms with intercourse. Counseling and education about safe sexual behaviors are critical to any successful prevention program for PID or other STDs.

## SCREENING AND RESCREENING

For women with symptomatic PID, it is too late to decrease their chances of having infertility or ectopic pregnancy or chronic pelvic pain, as antibiotic therapy does not change their risks of developing one of these chronic complications. The only way to prevent the complications of PID is to identify the infection before a woman develops symptomatic PID. Since chlamydia develops without symptoms in 70 percent of infected women, screening and identifying the infection early is the best way to prevent chronic complications of PID. Moreover, in a well-designed research study, researchers were able to successfully decrease cases of PID by 60 percent in populations of women who were screened regularly for chlamydia.

Programs that are effective in decreasing total numbers of chlamydia cases (and to a lesser extent, gonorrhea cases) within a population must include screening of high-risk individuals for asymptomatic infection. The CDC has suggested the following guidelines for screening women at high risk for chlamydia:

1. Annually screen all sexually active women 25 years of age or younger

2. Screen other high-risk women (single, African American, prior history of an STD, new or multiple sexual partners, inconsistent use of condoms)

3. Screen all pregnant women 25 years of age or younger

4. Screen high-risk pregnant women

Screening of men without any symptoms has not been recommended, as there is not enough evidence to suggest that

(*continued on page 67*)

## STD PREVENTION

The Centers for Disease Control and Prevention (CDC) has one branch devoted to sexually transmitted disease (STD) prevention efforts. This branch performs many important and critical public health tasks. A few examples of these tasks include tracking the numbers of cases of reportable sexually transmitted diseases that occur in the United States each year; overseeing an ongoing surveillance project that collects *N. gonorrhoeae* specimens from STD clinic patients across the country and tests the bacterial isolates for new types of resistance to antibiotics; and providing physicians and other healthcare providers who diagnose and treat patients with STDs with updated published guidelines on the treatment of STDs. Numerous other important projects are also coordinated by this branch of the CDC.

The federal government is not the only branch that provides important public health functions. Each city or county has a local health department, each of which reports to their respective state health department. The state health departments in turn report to the CDC. Local city and county health departments collect and coordinate reporting information from various clinical laboratories and doctors about new STD cases. However, the most important function of the local health department is provision of medical care for patients with possible STDs. All cities and/or counties with a certain number of citizens are required by the federal government to provide free confidential health care for all patients with a potential STD. These STD clinics serve as an invaluable resource and are the front line in the ongoing fight to identify, treat, and eradicate STDs in their communities.

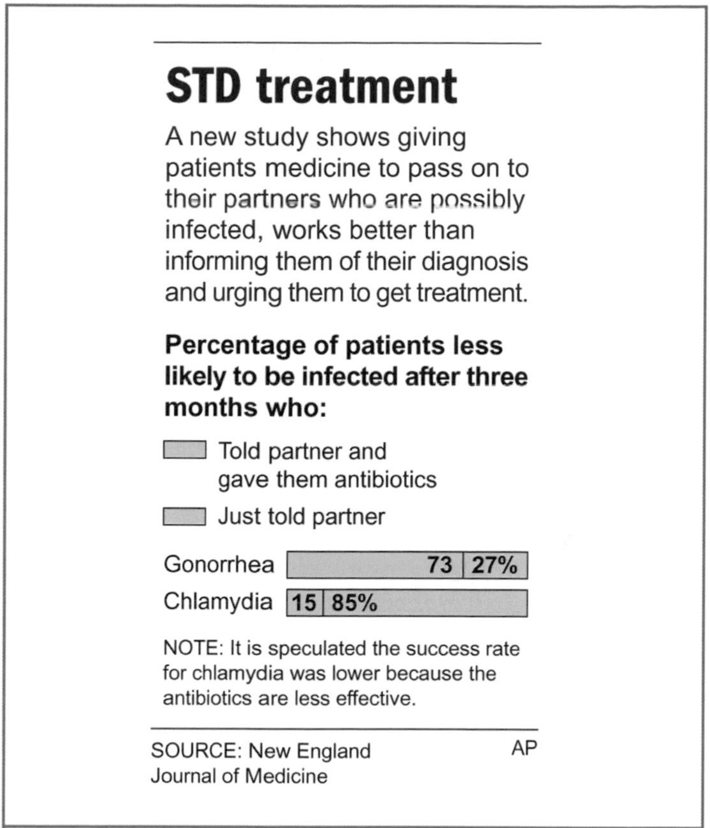

# STD treatment

A new study shows giving patients medicine to pass on to their partners who are possibly infected, works better than informing them of their diagnosis and urging them to get treatment.

**Percentage of patients less likely to be infected after three months who:**

▭ Told partner and
  gave them antibiotics

▭ Just told partner

| | | |
|---|---|---|
| Gonorrhea | 73 | 27% |
| Chlamydia | 15 | 85% |

NOTE: It is speculated the success rate for chlamydia was lower because the antibiotics are less effective.

SOURCE: New England                    AP
Journal of Medicine

**Figure 7.1  STD treatment.** © AP Graphics

*(continued from page 65)*

such a program would be effective in decreasing chlamydia rates.

There is a high frequency of repeat chlamydia infections within the first several months of the initial infection, especially in adolescents. Consequently, adolescents may need to be screened every six months for these repeat infections to be identified and treated before they cause upper genital tract infection.

## PARTNER TREATMENT

Many adolescent women have repeated chlamydial infections. Often this is because their partner or partners were not effectively treated and were thus able to reinfect them. Any successful program to prevent PID must have specific guidelines for partner notification and treatment. Most often patients with an STD are asked to notify their sexual partners that they may have been exposed to an STD and inform them that they should go to their doctor to get treated. When this type of notification is not feasible, however, the local health department can sometimes notify partners. Less commonly, patients may be given antibiotic therapy for their partner to take. This strategy is controversial; it is actually illegal in some states for physicians to give prescription medication to a patient for distribution to another person. No matter what the strategy, partners must receive treatment even if they feel fine and have no symptoms. Only with some mechanism to ensure appropriate and timely partner treatment can prevention of PID be successful.

**abscess**—An accumulation of pus in a defined space that results from an infection.

**acute**—Marked by sharpness or severity; also used to describe events that occur quickly.

**adnexa**—The area in the female pelvis where the ovary and top portion of the fallopian tube sit. Women have two adnexa, one on the left side and one on the right.

**anaerobes**—A specific group of bacteria that cannot survive in the presence of oxygen.

**asymptomatic**—Having or exhibiting no symptoms despite having a medical problem.

**cervical os**—The opening in the middle of the cervix that leads into the uterine canal and up into the cavity of the uterus.

**cervicitis**—Inflammation of the cervix.

**cervix**—The lower part of the uterus (womb) that connects with the top of the vagina.

**chlamydia**—The most common sexually transmitted disease in the United States; caused by *chlamydia trachomatis*. It is easily treated with antibiotics, though it can cause scarring and inflammation that lead to pelvic inflammatory disease.

***Chlamydia trachomatis***—The bacteria that causes chlamydia; it is treatable with antibiotics, but left untreated can contribute to pelvic inflammatory disease and blindness.

**chronic**—Long-lasting; a term used to describe events that occur later in the course of an illness and that may be present for a prolonged period of time.

**coccus (pl., cocci)**—A bacterium that is round in shape.

**computed tomography or CT scan**—A procedure that uses narrow beams of radiation to produce images of the body from different angles and then combines them for a precise view.

**conjunctivae**—Pink-colored tissue or membrane that covers the upper and lower lids.

**conjunctivitis**—Inflammation of the conjunctivae.

**ectocervix**—The outer, exposed portion of the cervix visible during a speculum examination, made up of distinct cells different from the inner portion of the cervix and uterus.

# Glossary

**ectopic pregnancy**—A pregnancy in which the fertilized egg does not implant itself in the uterus as it should, but rather implants itself on other organs or structures in the female pelvis. All such pregnancies cannot be sustained, since the fertilized egg cannot obtain nutrients from the mother.

**elementary body**—One of the two forms of *Chlamydia trachomatis*; this is the infectious form that can be transmitted from person to person.

**endocervix**—The inner portion of the cervix, made up of cells distinct from the ectocervix, but similar to the cells of the uterus.

**endometritis**—Inflammation of the lining of the uterus.

**epidemic**—Widespread infection of disease throughout a population.

**epididymis**—The small organ that sits above the testicles within the scrotum of men, and through which sperm travels.

**epididymitis**—Inflammation of the epididymis.

**fimbriae**—Finger-like protrusions at the end of the fallopian tubes.

**Fitz-Hugh-Curtis syndrome**—A rare acute complication of PID in which the capsule of the liver becomes infected and inflamed. Women with this syndrome complain of right-sided abdominal pain and are often mistakenly thought to have gallbladder problems or inflammation of the liver (hepatitis).

**flora**—Term used to describe the many different strains of bacteria that normally live on or in the human body; for example, there are bacteria that live on the skin, in the mouth and throat, and in the bowels. These bacteria are usually not harmful to humans, though in certain circumstances they can cause infection.

**Glisson's capsule**—The term for the capsule, or tissue cover, of the liver.

**Gram-negative bacteria**—Bacteria that appear red when stained with Gram's stain.

**Gram-positive bacteria**—Bacteria that appear purple when stained with Gram's stain.

**hepatitis**—Inflammation of the liver.

**human papillomaviruses**—Sexually transmitted viruses that cause genital warts and some forms of cancer in both men and women.

**hysterectomy**—Surgical procedure in which the uterus of a woman is removed from the body.

**imaging**—The action or process of producing an image, especially of a part of the body, by radiographic techniques.

**infertility**—Inability to reproduce (have children).

*in vitro* **fertilization**—A process through which a pregnancy is achieved by the removal of an egg from a woman and sperm from a man; the egg is fertilized in a laboratory and then returned to the woman for implantation in the uterus.

**labia majora**—The outer layer of tissue that surrounds and protects the vaginal opening.

**labia minora**—The inner layer of tissue, flatter and firmer than the labia majora, surrounding the vaginal opening.

**laparoscopy**—An invasive medical procedure in which a physician makes small incisions in the abdominal wall and inserts a thin tube with a light and video camera on the end of it into the abdominal cavity. Once inside the abdominal cavity, the physician can maneuver the scope and the camera can send pictures of various organs and other internal structures to a television screen.

**lithotomy position**—The position used for pelvic examinations, in which a woman lies on her back with her feet in stirrups and her knees spread apart.

**lymphomagranuloma venereum (LGV)**—Infection caused by serovars L1, L2, and L3 of *Chlamydia trachomatis* manifesting as swollen, painful lymph nodes with or without proctitis.

**menses**—The regular release of the endometrium, the lining of the uterus, as part of the menstrual cycle.

***Neisseria gonorrhoeae***—The bacteria that causes gonorrhea, a spherical bacteria that is always grouped in pairs.

**nucleic acid amplification tests (NAATs)**—Medical tests that identify specific nucleic acid sequences (nucleic acids are the building blocks of DNA) in clinical specimens and then reproduce them many times in order to identify and confirm their presence.

**ocular trachoma**—Infection of the eye that can lead to blindness caused by the serovars of *Chlamydia trachomatis* A, B, Ba, and C.

**oophorectomy**—A surgical procedure in which the ovaries of a woman are removed from the body.

# Glossary

**ovulation**—The release of eggs from the ovary for purposes of fertilization.

**palpate**—A medical term that means to press in on, and feel, a particular area of the body.

**Papanicolaou (Pap) smear**—A medical test in which the surface of the woman's cervix is gently scraped to collect cells. The sample is then stained with a special staining technique and examined under a microscope by a trained physician (i.e., pathologist) looking for abnormal or cancerous cervical cells.

**pathologist**—A doctor who specializes in diagnosing diseases by studying cells and tissues.

**pelvic inflammatory disease (PID)**—Infection of the upper female genital tract.

**perineum**—The external genital area, particularly the space between the vagina and the rectum.

**peritonitis**—Inflammation of the lining of the abdominal and pelvic cavities.

**pili (singular, pilus)**—Hair-like structures that extend out from the surface of the cell wall of a bacterium and usually help the bacterium to attach and stick to human cells.

**proctitis**—Inflammation of the anus and rectum.

**reportable disease**—A disease that must be reported to public health authorities when it is diagnosed.

**reticulate body**—One of two forms of *Chlamydia trachomatis*; this is the form capable of reproducing itself within the human host cell and completing the life cycle of the bacterium.

**rod**—A bacterium that is elongated or tubular in shape.

**salpingitis**—Inflammation of the ovaries and fallopian tubes.

**serovar**—Microbiologic term used to describe different strains or types of particular bacteria.

**sexually transmitted disease (STD)**—A disease transmitted through sexual contact.

**speculum**—A medical instrument used in the examination of the female pelvis. The speculum is inserted into the vagina and gently opened to allow the medical professional to visualize the patient's vagina and cervix.

**stricture**—Scar tissue in a man's urethra caused by gonorrhea; it may interfere with urination and ejaculation.

**transducer**—A medical instrument that acts as a transmitter and receiver of ultrasound information.

**trichomoniasis**—Sexually transmitted parasitic infection caused by *Trichomonas vaginalis,* usually treatable with antibiotics.

**ulcer**—A deep, open sore.

**ultrasound**—The use of ultrasonic waves for diagnostic or therapeutic purposes, specifically to image an internal body structure, monitor a developing fetus, or generate localized deep heat to the tissues.

**urethra**—The urinary canal, located in front of the lower portion of the vagina.

**urethritis**—Inflammation of the uterus, most often due to infection; symptoms include pain and burning sensation with urination.

**vaginitis**—Inflammation of the vulva due to infection, accompanied by pain, itching, and discharge.

**vector**—A medical term used to describe an object or thing that can transmit infection; for example, the mosquito is a vector for malaria.

# Bibliography

Centers for Disease Control and Prevention. *Sexually Transmitted Disease Surveillance 2003*. Atlanta, Ga.: Division of Sexually Transmitted Diseases, National Center for HIV, STD, and TB Prevention, 2004.

Centers for Disease Control and Prevention. *Sexually Transmitted Disease Surveillance 2003: Chlamydia Prevalence Monitoring Project*. Atlanta, Ga.: U.S. Department of Health and Human Services, 2005.

Centers for Disease Control and Prevention. *Sexually Transmitted Disease Surveillance 2003: Gonococcal Isolate Surveillance Project (GISP) Annual Report, 2003*. Atlanta, Ga.: U.S. Department of Health and Human Services, 2005.

Centers for Disease Control and Prevention. *Sexually Transmitted Disease Treatment Guidelines 2002*. MMWR 51, no. RR-6 (2002).

Eng, Thomas R., and William T. Butler, eds. *The Hidden Epidemic: Confronting Sexually Transmitted Diseases*. Washington, D.C.: National Academies Press, 1997.

Handsfield, H. H., and J. F. Sparling. "Neisseria gonorrhoeae." *Principles and Practice of Infectious Disease*. 6th ed. Gerald L. Mandell, John E. Bennett, and Raphael Dolin, eds. Philadelphia, Pa.: Elsevier Churchill Livingstone, 2005: 2514–2528.

Johnson, R.E., et al. "Screening tests to detect *C. trachomatis* and *N. gonorrhoeae* infections—2002." *MMWR Recommended Reports* 51 (2002): 1–38.

Marr, Lisa. *Sexually Transmitted Diseases: A Physician Tells You What You Need to Know*. Baltimore, Md.: Johns Hopkins University Press, 1999.

Stamm, W. E., R. B. Jones, and B. E. Baetteiger. "Chlamydia trachomatis." *Mandell, Douglas and Bennett's Principles and Practice of Infectious Disease*. 6th ed. Gerald L. Mandell, John E. Bennett, and Raphael Dolin, eds. Philadelphia, Pa.: Elsevier Churchill Livingstone, 2005: 2239–2255.

# Index

abdominal discomfort
  acute complication of
    PID, 34, 35
  chronic complication of
    PID, 42
  diminishing of, 32
  peritonitis and, 34
  symptom of PID, 9–10,
    23, 24
abscess
  acute complication of
    PID, 12, 34
  draining of, 32–33, 34
  fallopian tube, 29, 31,
    32
  ovarian, 24, 28, 29, 31,
    32
  rupture of, 34
  ultrasound identifica-
    tion of, 30
acquired immune defi-
  ciency syndrome
  (AIDS)
  blood test for, 11
  new disease, 6
  resistance to drugs, 7
  unprotected sex and, 50
acute complications of
  PID, 34–35. See also
  specific complication
acute urethral syndrome,
  61
adnexa
  tenderness, 29, 32
  upper female genital
    tract, 15, 17
adnexal tenderness, 29, 32
agar plate, 53–54
age
  chlamydia rates by, 59,
    60
  gonorrhea rates by, 50
  and infertility, 39
  PID, 60, 64
AIDS. See acquired
  immune deficiency
  syndrome

alcohol abuse, 39
anaerobes, 19, 22–23
anaerobic bacteria. See
  anaerobes
anal sex, 48
anatomy of PID, 15–19
anorexia, 39
antibiotic
  Neisseria gonorrhoeae
    resistance to, 43,
    44–45
  treatment with, 12,
    31–32, 33
antiretroviral drugs, 7
asymptomatic
  chlamydia, 30
  defined, 15
  gonorrhea, 30
  PID, 19
asymptomatic PID. See
  silent PID

bacteria culture
  for chlamydia, 62–63
  for gonorrhea, 53–54
bacteriology. See also
  specific bacteria
  Chlamydia trachomatis,
    55–63
  Neisseria gonorrhoeae,
    43–54
  of PID, 19–23, 31
behavioral prevention
  strategies, 64–65
bimanual examination,
  25, 26, 28
biology of PID, 19–23
birth control pill, 10, 60
birth defects, 40
bleeding, 23
blindness, 55
blood test, 11–12, 13
bulimia, 39

cancer cells, 27
case study, 8–14

CDC. See Centers for
  Disease Control and
  Prevention
cells, cancerous, 27
Centers for Disease
  Control and
  Prevention (CDC)
  reporting diseases to,
    49, 54
  screening recommenda-
    tions for chlamydia,
    61, 65
  and STD prevention,
    33, 66
cephalosporins, 45
cervical motion tender-
  ness, 29, 32
cervicitis
  chlamydia and, 61
  defined, 18, 19
  symptoms of, 24, 52
cervix
  bacterium growth in, 19
  discharge from, 24, 25
  cancerous cells in, 27
  cervical motion tender-
    ness, 29, 32
  examination of, 11, 25
  infection of, 21, 52
  infertility and, 39
  inflammation of, 18, 19,
    25
  lower female genital
    tract, 15, 17
chlamydia
  causes of, 21–23, 31
  clinical illnesses caused
    by, 62
  common cause of PID,
    19
  diagnosis and treat-
    ment, 13–14, 25, 30,
    33, 62–63
  frequency of repeat
    infections, 67
  incidence of and risk
    factors for, 59–61

# Index

infection targets, 17
infertility and, 37, 42
microbiology of
*Chlamydia trachomatis*, 57–59
prevention strategies, 64–68
rates by age, 59, 60
rates by race and ethnicity, 60
rates of infection, 59
symptoms, 60–61
transmission of, 59
*Chlamydia trachomatis.*
*See also* chlamydia
clinical illnesses caused by, 62
defined, 21
diagnosis of, 62–63
first identified, 55
in Fitz-Hugh-Curtis syndrome, 34
incidence of and risk factors for, 59–61
microbiology of, 57–59
proctitis caused by, 53
silent epidemic, 56–57
transmission of, 59
vaccine development, 64
cholera, 6
chronic complications of PID, 34, 35–42, 65. *See also specific complication*
clinical presentation of PID, 23–24
coccus (*pl.* cocci), 46
complications of PID. *See also specific complication*
acute, 34–35
chronic, 34, 35–42, 65
computed tomography. *See* CT scan
condom, use of, 10, 65

conjunctivae, 20
conjunctivitis
chlamydia and infants, 62
symptom of gonorrhea and, 20, 53
cryptosporidiosis, 6
CT scan
described, 30
in diagnosing Fitz-Hugh-Curtis syndrome, 35
for fallopian or ovary abscess, 32, 33
culture, 53–54, 62–63

DDT, 6
diagnosing
chlamydia, 13–14, 25, 30, 33, 62–63
*Chlamydia trachomatis*, 62–63
fallopian or ovarian abscess, 32, 33
Fitz-Hugh-Curtis syndrome, 35
gonorrhea, 25, 30, 33, 53–54
PID, 10–12, 28–31
diphtheria, 6
diplococci, 46
drug
abuse, 39
exposure to certain, 40
use and gonorrhea, 51

eating disorders and ovulation, 39
ectocervix, 17, 52
ectopic pregnancy
age and at-risk conditions, 60
chronic complication of PID, 40–42
defined, 37

screening for infections and, 65
education and gonorrhea, 51
eggs, 15, 17
elementary body, 58
endocervix, 17, 52, 53
endometriosis, 39–40
endometritis, 18, 62
epidemic, 56
epididymis, 19
epididymitis, 21, 52, 61
ethnicity
and chlamydia rates, 60
and gonorrhea rates, 50–51
examination for PID, 10–12, 25–28
eye infections. *See also* conjunctivitis
and chlamydia, 62
and gonorrhea, 20, 53

fallopian tubes
abscess, 29, 31, 32
damage to, 15, 39–40
examination of, 11
inflammation of, 18, 36–37
infertility, 38
scarring, 14, 19, 21, 36
upper female genital tract, 15, 17
female genital tract
lower, 15, 16–17, 24
terms to describe infections, 18
upper, 15, 17, 19, 21, 61–62
female infertility, 39. *See also* infertility
fever
acute complication of PID, 35
hospitalization for, 31

# Index

microscope, invention of, 7

Motrin®, 32

NAATs. *See* nucleic acid amplification tests

nausea
  acute complication of PID, 9–10, 24, 35
  disappearing of, 32
  hospitalization for, 31
  minor complaint of, 23

Navajo Nation, 6

Neisser, Albert, 43

*Neisseria gonorrhoeae. See also* gonorrhea
  bacteriology of gonorrhea, 19–21
  clinical illnesses caused by, 51–53
  first identified, 43
  in Fitz-Hugh-Curtis syndrome, 34
  incidence of and risk factors for, 48–51
  microbiology of, 46–48
  resistance to antibiotics, 43, 44–45
  testing for resistance to antibiotics, 66
  transmission of, 48
  vaccine development, 64

nucleic acid amplification tests (NAATs)
  in diagnosing chlamydia, 63
  in diagnosing gonorrhea, 54

obesity, 39

ocular trachoma, 55

oophorectomy, 42

oral contraceptives and chlamydia, 60

oral sex and transmission of gonorrhea, 48, 53

os, 17, 52

outpatient treatment, 31

ovaries
  abscess, 24, 28, 29, 31, 32, 34
  damage to, 15
  examination of, 11
  inflammation of, 18

oophorectomy, 42

upper female genital tract, 15, 17

ovulation, 39

pain relief, 32

palpates, 26

Papanicolaou, George, 27

Pap smear
  described, 25–26
  detection of cervical cancer, 57
  history of, 27

partner
  limiting number of, 64
  treatment of, 13–14, 33, 67–68

pathologist, 25

pelvic examination
  in case study, 11
  described, 25–28
  in diagnosing chlamydia, 63

pelvic inflammatory disease (PID)
  age and at-risk conditions, 60, 64
  anatomy of, 15–19
  biology and bacteriology of, 19–23
  case study, 8–14
  clinical presentation of, 23–24
  complications of PID, 34–42

diagnosis, 10–12, 28–31

examination, 10–12, 25–28

management of, 12, 31–33

partner treatment, 67–68

prevention strategies, 64–65

screening and rescreening, 65, 67

symptoms of, 8–10, 12–13, 23–24, 28–29

pelvic pain, chronic, 42, 65

pelvis, 17

penicillin, 43, 44

penis, 19, 20

perineum, 16

peritoneum, 34

peritonitis, 34, 62

pesticides, 6

pharyngeal gonorrhea, 53

physical examination, 25–28

pneumonia, 6

PID. *See* pelvic inflammatory disease

pilus (*pl.* pili), 47

plasmid, 44–45

polio, 6

polyps, 39

pregnancy
  chlamydia and, 62
  fallopian tube scarring, 14
  gonorrhea and, 48
  test, 12

prevention strategies, 64–65

proctitis, 21, 53

pus
  in cervix, 25
  in ovarian abscess, 28, 34

# Index

vaginitis, 18, 52
vomiting. *See* nausea

warts, genital, 57
WBCs. *See* white blood cells

West Nile virus, 6
white blood cells (WBCs)
  elevation in, 29
  fallopian tubes and, 37

whooping cough, 6
womb. *See* uterus

yeast infections, 18

**Judith A. O'Donnell, M.D.**, received her B.S. in Biology from the University of Scranton and her M.D. from Temple University School of Medicine. She completed her residency training in internal medicine, as well as her Infectious Diseases fellowship training, at Temple University Hospital. She is board certified in both internal medicine and infectious diseases, and her clinical practice is solely in the specialty of infectious diseases. She is currently an associate professor of medicine in the Division of Infectious Diseases, Department of Medicine, at Drexel University College of Medicine in Philadelphia, where she has been a faculty member for 12 years. Dr. O'Donnell serves as the Director of the Infectious Diseases fellowship-training program at Drexel University College of Medicine and is responsible for the training and education of those physicians interested in subspecialty training in the field of infectious diseases. She lectures to medical students, residents, and fellows on a variety of infectious disease topics, including sexually transmitted diseases (STDs). Dr. O'Donnell previously served as the Medical Director of the STD Control Program and the STD Clinic at the Philadelphia Department of Public Health. She was one of four national awardees for a five-year grant from the Centers of Disease Control and Prevention (CDC) for improving STD education among medical students and in post-graduate medical training programs. She is an author of several peer-reviewed journal articles in the medical literature as well as many book chapters.

**Steven P. Gelone, PharmD.**, received his B.S. in Pharmacy and his doctorate in Pharmacy from Temple University School of Pharmacy. He was previously a tenured associate professor of pharmacy, as well as the Director of Clinical Research, the Director of the Infectious Disease and Clinical Research fellowship programs at Temple University School of Pharmacy, where he was a faculty member for 11 years. During his time at the Temple School of Pharmacy he also served as the Director of Clinical Pharmacology at the National Institute of Health-funded General Clinical Research Center at Temple University Hospital. Dr. Gelone is the author of numerous peer-reviewed articles and book chapters in the medical and pharmacy literature. He has held several positions of increasing responsibility in the pharmaceutical industry in clinical pharmacology and medical affairs. He is currently the President of *Cmax* Consultants, a clinical development and medical affairs consulting firm located in Wyndmoor, Pennsylvania.